Contents

The Manager's Guide to Discipline

Derek Eccleston and
Kate Goschen

GOWER

Published by
Gower Publishing Limited
Gower House
Croft Road
Aldershot
Hampshire GU11 3HR
England

Gower Publishing Company
Suite 420
101 Cherry Street
Burlington, VT 05401-4405
USA

www.gowerpublishing.com

British Library Cataloguing in Publication Data
Eccleston, Derek
    The manager's guide to discipline
    1. Labor discipline 2. Personnel management
    I. Title II. Goschen, Kate
    658.3'14

    ISBN: 978-0-566-08855-1

Library of Congress Cataloging-in-Publication Data
Eccleston, Derek.
    The manager's guide to discipline / by Derek Eccleston and Kate Goschen.
       p. cm.
    Includes index.
    ISBN 978-0-566-08855-1
    1. Labor discipline. 2. Personnel management. I. Goschen, Kate. II. Title.

    HF5549.5.L3E33 2008
    658.3'14--dc22

                                                                2008016614

Mixed Sources
Product group from well-managed forests and other controlled sources
www.fsc.org Cert no. SGS-COC-2482
© 1996 Forest Stewardship Council

Printed and bound in Great Britain by
TJ International Ltd, Padstow, Cornwall.

Acknowledgements

Thanks are due to a number of people who have helped in the production of this guide. The original idea for this work sprang from a request from one of my clients, Susie Ward at Spitfire Technology, who requested a best practice guide for managers at her company. Thank you for asking, Susie!

Many thanks also to Kate Morrison who kindly took the time to read and comment on this in draft form, providing honest feedback from a 'line manager' perspective.

Finally, my thanks to Kate Goschen for invaluable support with the writing and proofing of the materials that make up this work.

Introduction

The use of disciplinary procedures is quite common in the UK, and surveys have suggested that between 3 per cent and 5 per cent of the working population receive some form of disciplinary sanction each year. This means around 50 disciplinary cases in an organisation of 1,000 employees.

So what should 'disciplinary action' be trying to achieve? There is a range of options:

(a) Retribution/punishment – disciplinary action is seen as a punishment for wrongdoing; typically this would be serious or gross misconduct often ending in dismissal.

(b) Deterrent/caution – disciplinary action is used to highlight the adverse consequences of future actions; perhaps a warning for breaching health and safety.

(c) Rehabilitation/corrective – disciplinary action is viewed as correctional and a training opportunity, typically poor performance or poor attendance issues.

A dictionary gives several other definitions of discipline before 'correction and chastisement':

- instruction

- imparting knowledge

- training

- a system of rules for performance or conduct.

Discipline therefore should *not normally* be seen as chastisement and punishment. In fact the ACAS Code (which can be downloaded or viewed at www.acas.org.uk) suggests that discipline is aimed at bringing about an improvement in an employee's conduct, performance or behaviour.

On occasions serious misconduct or gross misconduct will justify a rapid move towards the termination of employment, but most cases of discipline and dismissal do not involve serious or gross misconduct. Whilst dismissals for issues like fighting or theft tend to grab the headlines, the most frequent reasons for embarking upon disciplinary action usually relate to offences involving poor attendance or failing to reach performance standards. However, in recent years the rapid growth of technology in the workplace, in particular access to the Internet, has led to a sharp increase in disciplinary offences for Internet related reasons.

Discipline should be about setting **standards** of behaviour and performance and letting staff know what those standards are. It is also about helping staff to achieve and maintain those standards by setting an example:

- through training

- through guidance

- through communication.

It is worthwhile remembering that management (in broad terms) has been responsible for the recruitment and/or promotion (and training) of these individuals who may now have performance problems.

The aim of this manual is to provide a practical insight into the handling of disciplinary and dismissal issues.

First of all, it is important to read this document in conjunction with your company's own 'Disciplinary Procedures'. **Tribunals always expect the employer to follow their Disciplinary Procedure closely**. (Appendix I provides a draft example of a Discipline Procedure, and Appendix II, an example of a Capability Procedure).

The policy should incorporate but expand upon any statutory dismissal and disciplinary procedures which are set out in the ACAS Code.

This Manager's Guide is a tool to assist you with putting the Company Disciplinary Procedures policy into practice, giving consideration to employment law and best practice. This not only covers the procedure in more detail, but also highlights the actions that need to be taken, the decisions that need to be made and the considerations managers need to take when making those decisions.

The appendices include checklists on how to prepare and conduct a disciplinary hearing and standard letters to help with the process. These should enable the company to demonstrate that not only has the policy been adhered to, but that there is a clear record showing what the circumstances were and how it was handled in the event of any dispute or tribunal claim.

1 The Basic Requirements

To be disciplined for an act of misconduct or poor performance can have a serious effect on the employee concerned. At best, it acts as a 'black mark' and at worst it could lead to dismissal. So a decision to take disciplinary action should not be taken lightly and procedures must be followed closely. Failure to follow the procedures and/or if the company have acted unreasonably in all the circumstances, will allow the employee to claim unfair dismissal before an employment tribunal – provided they have one year's continuous service.

Disciplinary rules and procedures are necessary for promoting orderly employment relations as well as fairness and consistency in the treatment of employees. They also enable companies to influence the conduct of employees and deal with problems of poor performance, thereby assisting companies to operate effectively. Rules set out standards of conduct and performance at work; procedures ensure the standards are adhered to and also provide a fair method of dealing with alleged failures to observe them. It is important that employees know what standards of conduct and performance are expected of them (and the consequences of not meeting them) before any disciplinary action can be taken, otherwise this will be deemed as unfair. This may be achieved by giving every employee a copy of the rules and by explaining them. In the case of new employees this should form part of the induction programme.

The Disciplinary Procedures should be applied consistently because an employment tribunal may view inconsistency without good reason as unfair.

A sound process will normally involve the following stages:

THE SIX STAGES OF DISCIPLINE

1. Investigation. Collect evidence. No action should be taken without taking time to check the facts. It is permissible to suspend an employee (normally *on full pay*) during an investigation – but only when serious or gross misconduct is suspected.

2. Invite the employee to a formal meeting, in writing. They can bring a companion – this is a statutory right at any formal meeting.

3. Adjourn before reaching a decision.

4. Further hearing(s) if necessary.

5. Decision, given in writing, confirming right to appeal.

6. Appeal – NB: generally very important.

DO I ALWAYS HAVE TO FOLLOW THIS PROCESS?

The right to claim unfair dismissal requires one year's continuous service as an employee. Strictly speaking therefore it is not *essential* to follow a full procedure where the employee has less than one year's service, as no claim for unfair dismissal is possible. However, claims for discrimination and breach of contract do not require a year's service, so care is still required when dismissing anyone (including casual staff), irrespective of service. See Appendix IV: Checklist 7 for more information on qualifying periods. If a probationary period is used for new employees it is advisable not to put the full company discipline scheme in their contract until probation has been satisfactorily concluded. A shorter process, perhaps giving just one warning prior to dismissal, can be used. This will reduce the chances of a breach of contract claim. Best practice is to always follow a basic procedure, as outlined above, to reduce the risk of a claim. It is also possible to justify not following a full procedure where the conduct of the employee continues to be unacceptable – aggressive, threatening, abusive and so on.

MANAGING AGENCY AND CASUAL STAFF

Case law has highlighted how important it is for companies to recognise who has responsibility for the management (and discipline) of agency staff.

A worker was engaged by an agency under a contract for services. The agency placed the worker with a large employer and he continued to work there, under this arrangement, for some time. The employer began experiencing problems with the worker's performance. The worker was disciplined, suspended and eventually dismissed by management at the large employer.

The Tribunal decided that the worker could claim unfair dismissal against the employer – not the agency. The way that the management had dealt with the worker had, in effect, created an *implied* employment relationship. A contract of employment can be *expressed* or *implied* – the courts are showing a willingness to *imply* a contract of employment where the facts suggest the relationship was like employment.

If organisations experience problems with agency workers, it is important to involve the agency in dealing with the issues. Do not treat agency workers as your own employees or the courts may give employment protection to them. It is important to remember that agency workers (not just employees) enjoy an increasing number of employment rights.

The message from the courts is that agency and casual arrangements are meant to be for weeks or months, not years.

AVOID PROBLEMS IN THE FIRST PLACE BY ESTABLISHING DISCIPLINARY RULES AND PROCEDURES

Disciplinary rules set down the standards that govern the behaviour of employees in the workplace (for example, no smoking, dress code, timekeeping). The procedures inform individuals as to what will happen if the expected levels of conduct or performance are not kept. Clear procedures make it easier for management to deal with poor performance and misconduct issues.

The Advisory Conciliation and Arbitration Service (ACAS) has issued a Code of Practice on handling discipline at work. Whilst this is not a legal requirement, it has heavy influence with tribunals. Anyone involved in disciplinary issues should have a working knowledge of this Code. The Code recommends a number of features for fair disciplinary procedures. A fair disciplinary procedure should:

(a) be in writing;

(b) specify to whom the procedure applies;

(c) provide for matters to be dealt with promptly;

(d) indicate the different disciplinary actions which may be taken;

(e) specify which levels of management have the authority to take the various forms of disciplinary action. It is good practice to ensure that first line supervisors do not normally have the power to dismiss without reference to senior management;

(f) provide for employees to be informed of complaints against them and to be given an opportunity to state their case before decisions are reached; it is recommended that an employee be informed *in writing* of the employer's concerns;

(g) give individuals the right to be accompanied by a trade union representative or a fellow employee of their choice. Since 2000, regulations have provided certain rights to workers (typically agency or casual staff). In the past these rights have only been available to employees – individuals who have a contract of employment. One of these new rights for workers is the right to be accompanied at disciplinary or grievance hearings. It is recommended that everyone is offered a companion – including casual workers and temporary staff who may not be classed as employees;

(h) ensure that, except in the case of gross misconduct, no employees are dismissed for a first breach of discipline;

(i) ensure that disciplinary action is not taken until the case has been thoroughly investigated;

(j) ensure that individuals are given a full explanation for any disciplinary penalty imposed;

(k) provide the right of appeal and specify how individuals are expected to appeal;

(l) ensure that all employees are aware of the offences that the employer considers as gross misconduct. A body of case law has made it clear that if an employee can allege that they were unaware that the offence committed was classed as gross misconduct, the Tribunal will consider that when making a decision.

Absence of any of the above features would be likely to cause an employer some difficulty if the case is referred to an employment tribunal.

In addition to the above features of a fair disciplinary procedure, employers should ensure that:

(a) the procedure applies to all employees irrespective of length of service – although, remember that to claim unfair dismissal an employee needs one year's continuous service;

(b) the procedure does not discriminate in any way;

(c) there is a provision to suspend (initially with full pay) employees during the investigation stage;

(d) where the facts themselves are in dispute, no disciplinary action is taken until the facts have been established.

Of course, the ACAS guide is quite literally that: a guide. The precise nature and content of disciplinary rules and procedures will always depend on a number of issues. These are:

- the type of work done at the establishment

- the working conditions prevailing

- the size of the establishment.

It is for each and every organisation to decide on the specific content of disciplinary rules and procedures. Certain offences can be more serious in some firms than others.

SETTING STANDARDS

For any disciplinary action to have a chance of a successful outcome, there are a number of essential ingredients.

These are:

(a) the organisation has a clear set of standards;

(b) the standards have been communicated to all workers;

(c) factual evidence is available which indicates that conduct or performance is below the accepted standard;

(d) there are clear rules and procedures, which outline to all employees how the issue will be dealt with.

This is a crucial concept. It is virtually impossible to bring about an improvement in someone's performance or conduct unless these elements are present. Unless a worker is prepared to acknowledge that they were aware of a standard, and there is clear evidence that they are below the standard, a successful conclusion is unlikely.

② Disciplinary Procedures in Operation

Should a manager decide to take disciplinary action against an employee, the golden rule is that the Company Disciplinary Procedures should always be followed.

The disciplinary procedures should not be viewed primarily as a means of punishment or of imposing sanctions, rather they should be seen as a way of helping and encouraging improvement amongst employees whose conduct or performance is unsatisfactory. With the possible exception of gross misconduct the approach should be to try to bring the employee up to the required standard of performance. Discipline should be more about improving conduct, behaviour or performance and less about punishment.

GROSS MISCONDUCT AND SUSPENSION FROM WORK

Gross misconduct is conduct so bad that it enables the employer to dismiss for a first offence (after following the process outlined the previous chapter). Never 'instantly'

13

dismiss any employee, it is likely to be considered as unfair). The disciplinary policy should give some examples of what constitutes gross misconduct. Some offences would be classed as gross misconduct in most organisations, for example fighting, theft and fraud. However, most businesses will also have other offences that they feel warrant dismissal. These should be listed as examples in the discipline procedure. It is also sensible to state that the list is not exhaustive to enable managers to deal with other offences of a similar nature that are not included in the list.

In a serious case such as gross misconduct, consideration must be given to a brief period of suspension from work (normally with full pay) whilst a full investigation is carried out. A short period of suspension may be helpful or necessary, although it should only be imposed after careful consideration and after an initial investigation and should be kept under review. Suspension should be for no longer than is reasonably necessary in the circumstances. There is no legal restriction on the length of a suspension. If the offence does not warrant suspending the employee, it may well be that this does not constitute gross misconduct and should therefore attract a warning prior to any dismissal.

If the manager has good reason to believe that an employee has committed an act of gross misconduct, they must take advice before taking the decision whether or not to suspend the employee. The timing of this decision is crucial. If the decision is to suspend the employee then this must be done immediately; in most cases the same day, so it is important for the manager to obtain the initial facts surrounding the case quickly in order to make this decision. Failure to suspend or to delay the decision and suspend at a later date could make a summary dismissal for gross misconduct unfair. If the employee was allowed to continue to work when they should have been suspended it raises the question whether the action of the employee was actually that bad and, therefore, did it constitute gross misconduct? As a minimum, they should be removed from the type of work normally done; so redeployed instead of an outright suspension from all work.

If the employee is to be suspended from work pending further investigation, this should be confirmed to them in writing (see Appendix III: Letter A).

INVESTIGATION

Where a disciplinary matter arises, the manager should first establish the facts promptly before recollections fade. A full investigation is necessary before a decision can be taken as to whether or not an employee deserves to be disciplined. The manager cannot act on the basis of mere suspicion and should treat matters of hearsay with great caution. The manager must have an honest and genuine belief, based on some proof (facts), following a reasonable investigation that the employee is guilty of the alleged misconduct or poor performance and that they were aware of the standard expected.

A thorough investigation is vital to a fair disciplinary process. Only then can the manager decide whether to drop the matter, arrange informal coaching or counselling or for the matter to be dealt with under the formal disciplinary procedures. Where the disciplinary offence relates to poor attendance, long term sickness, or possibly poor performance where ill health is a factor, medical advice should be sought as part of the investigation. This can range from seeking a report from the employee's doctor (which requires the employee's consent) through to involving Occupational Health or a referral to a specialist.

The manager must undertake an investigation at the earliest opportunity, as soon as they become aware of the facts. Failure to act promptly may allow the employee to claim unfair dismissal, since to be aware of the conduct and to do nothing may be viewed as the manager's acceptance that such conduct or performance is permitted.

In conducting the investigation, the manager must meet with the employee to obtain the facts (See Appendix III: Letter B) and any written statements should be signed by the employee. This is not a disciplinary hearing (and must not be conducted as one) and it should be made clear to the employee that this is the case. There is no legal right for the employee to have a companion in this type of meeting, but if it is felt that it would help, do not unreasonably refuse this, particularly if the employee has a disability, language problems or is a young worker (under 18).

Note: Where two or more employees are suspected of misconduct and the employer, despite investigation, cannot discover who is to blame, it may be fair to dismiss several employees in relation to the same incident without the dismissal being unfair.

All witnesses (if necessary) should be interviewed and statements taken and signed. It is important to have somewhere private to do this so that details can be obtained properly. Witnesses should be informed that the statement they provide may be seen by the employee and that they may be asked to attend the disciplinary hearing. The employee is allowed to do this in order to test the accuracy of the witness' account of events or to establish whether there is any ulterior motive for the allegation. The problem is complicated where the witness then wishes to remain anonymous. This can put the employee at the centre of the allegation at a potential disadvantage and makes it difficult for the manager to substantiate the allegation. In such situations employment tribunals have provided the following guidelines to ensure a fair hearing whilst protecting the request for anonymity, which managers must follow:

- The witness' statement should be written in full.

- In taking the statement the manager must note the date, time and place of each observation or incident.

- The manager should consider whether the witness had any reason to fabricate evidence.

- Having taken the statement, the manager should undertake further investigation with a view to finding other independent supporting evidence.

- Enquiries should be made into the character and background of the witness.

- A decision must then be made as to whether to hold a disciplinary hearing.

- If possible, the witness should be personally interviewed by the manager with a view to deciding what weight should be given to their evidence.

- The witness' statement should be made available to the employee and their representative in advance of the disciplinary hearing.

- Should the employee or their representative have any reasonable questions to ask the witness, wherever practicable the manager should accommodate a request and refer back with answers.

- Careful notes should be taken at the disciplinary hearing where witnesses are involved.

The investigation may lead the manager to look at other areas to link the allegation with what the witnesses are saying (for example, written evidence of poor performance, relevant paperwork such as timesheets, emails, CCTV footage, and so on). The manager must ensure that the investigation is not targeted or limited to find the employee guilty but seeks out other relevant areas to provide a balanced and informed view.

Once the investigation has been completed and the facts established the manager must write to the employee confirming the decision whether or not to convene a disciplinary hearing (See Appendix III: Letters C and D). In the case of a formal disciplinary hearing all facts of the investigation must be provided in the letter.

Although it is extremely important to conduct a thorough investigation, the manager should not unnecessarily delay the disciplinary hearing. There is a balance to be struck between having possession of most of the facts and acting promptly. Where the period of investigation is seen to be unnecessarily lengthy and the employee is subsequently dismissed, a claim for unfair dismissal may be possible if the employee can show, for example, that the statements were stale or witnesses were not available.

There are no hard and fast rules as to who should carry out the investigation. For the process to be seen to be fair, there are times when the manager is not the appropriate person to be both judge and jury. In such situations, an independent investigating officer could be appointed, or alternatively if the manager is involved in the investigation, a separate manager should conduct the disciplinary hearing and make the decision. This needs to be clearly impartial. Situations that may warrant this more objective approach include;

- The manager is also a witness to misconduct.

- The employee has complained about the manager, perhaps with a grievance.

- There is a history of relationship problems.

Conduct that occurs outside of the workplace can still justify a dismissal. However, the conduct must be of particular relevance to the job in question (or be shown to have genuinely brought the employer into disrepute). In relation to criminal charges an employer will still be required to conduct a full and thorough investigation which may include suspension of the employee. It is not necessary to refrain from any such action until the outcome of the criminal proceedings is known; indeed such a delay could render a potentially fair dismissal unfair. However, it is extremely important that an employer carries out their own investigation, and the offence must be shown to relate in some way back to work.

INFORMAL VERBAL WARNING

Cases of minor misconduct or unsatisfactory performance are usually best dealt with informally by the manager. A private meeting should be held between the manager and the employee to discuss the issue and a way forward agreed, including, where appropriate, the standard expected, timescale to improve and support provided. A record of the meeting should be held by the manager for future reference. This should be a file or diary note and not a formal letter to the employee.

Some organisations now refer to this type of meeting as a counselling meeting. In the face of a general reluctance to say to people that they have been given an informal warning, it is perhaps seen as being rather more user-friendly to describe such a meeting as counselling, precautionary or advisory. It is up to the supervisor or manager to decide how many informal or counselling meetings will be held. In most situations, one or two will be enough either to bring about an improvement, or will be sufficient to form the impression that more formal action is required.

There are no legal guidelines as to how long informal warnings should last. However, a period of two or three months would be reasonable – and the minimum recommended is a month. If performance or conduct has not improved within this period, the manager will rightly consider a more formal approach, for example, using the official warnings process.

> For further information on the significant differences between Informal and Formal Disciplinary situations refer to Appendix IV: Checklist 1.

FORMAL DISCIPLINARY ACTION

Where matters are more serious or where informal warnings have not been successful, managers should consider taking formal disciplinary action.

CAPABILITY OR CONDUCT?

Employment law provides just six potentially fair reasons for dismissal.

These reasons are:

1. The employees' conduct.

2. The employees' capability.

3. The job is redundant (i.e. the job no longer exists or is being relocated).

4. The dismissal is required by statute, such as someone working illegally.

5. A planned retirement as allowed for in the Age Discrimination Regulations.

6. Some other substantial reason justifying dismissal (SOSR); perhaps imprisonment, terminating a fixed term contract or bringing the employer into disrepute.

It is clear that the issues of capability and conduct are treated as separate offences justifying dismissal. The ACAS Code also makes it very clear that no one should be dismissed for their first offence, unless this offence constitutes gross misconduct.

It is therefore very important for supervisors and line managers to recognise the difference between a warning for someone's capability and a warning for someone's conduct. Case law has indicated that employers who fail to recognise the distinction between capability and conduct are much more likely to incur an unfair dismissal.

To simplify matters:

(a) Conduct – **won't** – this is where the individual **will not** work to the standards required; examples are timekeeping, theft, fighting and not following health and safety rules.

(b) Capability – **can't** – this is where the worker **cannot** achieve the standards required.

Examples include long term sickness, absence, lack of a qualification and poor performance due to a lack of ability.

Two sample policies are provided in the Appendices, one covering discipline (or misconduct) and the other capability.

There is no legal requirement to have separate policies, but it is increasingly seen as good practice. Where only one policy is in use, the disciplining officer needs to be aware whether this is a capability or conduct issue. If it is a conduct offence, current warnings for misconduct are relevant. However, current warnings for capability should not be taken into consideration, as they are separate offences. An employee could therefore have two formal warnings running at the same time, one for capability, one for misconduct.

DETAILS OF THE ALLEGATION

The employee should have sight of the evidence and understand the case against them well in advance of the disciplinary hearing. This is to allow them to prepare and present a defence. It is reasonable to allow the employee a *minimum* of two working days' notice of a disciplinary hearing in order for them to do this. However, it may be reasonable to provide additional notice if there is a lot of evidence for the employee to consider, or dismissal is contemplated.

The evidence should be sent accompanied by the letter notifying the employee of a disciplinary hearing (See Appendix III: Letter D). A disciplinary hearing must take place before any decision is made or any other penalty is imposed on the employee.

Once the employee has been given the details there should be no new allegations added at the disciplinary hearing. If that should occur, the employee would be acting reasonably in declining to comment and requesting an adjournment in order to review their defence. The allegations and their specific facts should be the focus of the disciplinary hearing.

THE RIGHT TO BE ACCOMPANIED

Employees have a right to be accompanied at a formal disciplinary hearing. Where an employee is required to attend a formal disciplinary hearing and requests a companion, the manager must allow either a trade union official or a fellow employee to attend. There is no legal right (unless this is allowed for in the discipline procedure or within indentures for an apprentice) for the employee to be accompanied by any other person, for example, a solicitor, friend or family member (unless they also happen to be a trade union official or a fellow employee).

However, always act reasonably and if the employee has a disability, problems with language, or they are a young worker, do consider allowing another companion, possibly a friend, to assist.

The accompanying person must be:

● Selected by the employee.

● Permitted to address the disciplinary hearing in order to do any or all of the following:

    – State the employee's case.
    – Sum up the case.
    – Respond on the employee's behalf to any view expressed at the disciplinary hearing.

● Permitted to confer with the employee during the disciplinary hearing.

However, the accompanying person has no right to answer questions on behalf of the employee, or to address the disciplinary hearing if the employee indicates that they do not wish the accompanying person to do so. (Hence the term *accompany* rather than *represent*).

While managers are free to select a date for a disciplinary hearing, there is a requirement to reschedule where the accompanying person is not available on that date. The employee must propose an alternative time which is reasonable and which falls within a period of five working days (excluding weekends and Bank Holidays), beginning with the first working day after the initial proposed date. If the accompanying person is a fellow employee, they must be given paid time off work during working hours to prepare for the meeting and to accompany the employee. Failure to observe this requirement may result in an employment tribunal awarding compensation to the employee of up to two weeks' pay.

WHAT IF A GRIEVANCE IS RAISED DURING A DISCIPLINARY CASE?

In the course of a disciplinary process, an employee may raise a grievance that is related to the case. If this happens, the manager should consider a short pause in the disciplinary procedure while the grievance is dealt with. Depending on the nature of the grievance, consider bringing in another manager to deal with the disciplinary process. In small organisations this may not be possible, and the existing manager should deal with the case as impartially as possible.

TRADE UNION REPRESENTATIVES

Disciplinary action against a trade union representative can lead to a serious dispute if it is seen as an attack on the union's functions. Normal standards apply but, if disciplinary action is considered, the matter should be discussed, after obtaining the employee's agreement, with a senior trade union representative or fulltime union official.

THE DISCIPLINARY HEARING

Appendix IV: Checklist 2: 'Preparation for a Disciplinary Hearing' should be used in the preparation of a disciplinary hearing and Appendix IV: Checklist 3: 'Carrying out a Disciplinary Hearing' should be used during the disciplinary hearing to ensure that all the points are covered.

The disciplinary hearing should be conducted promptly as delays may result in the employee's (and witnesses') recollection of events becoming dim and prevent them from providing a satisfactory explanation. Not unlike the investigation, unreasonable delay may result in a finding of unfair dismissal by a tribunal. In addition, the requirement under ACAS guidelines is that each step and action must be taken without unreasonable delay.

Note: if the employee fails to turn up for the hearing, the meeting should be adjourned to find out the reason. Avoid the temptation to press on and deal with the matter in their absence. A second meeting should be convened, and the employee can be informed that a second failure to appear (without good cause) may result in action being taken at that meeting. It is quite high risk to dismiss someone in their absence and every effort should be made to encourage the employee to attend.

A manager should chair the hearing and ideally there should also be a minute-taker present. Tape recording the hearing is permissible in certain circumstances, provided the employee is informed in advance.

The disciplinary hearing should take place during working hours, but not left until right at the end of the day or the week. It is sensible to hold a disciplinary hearing either at the beginning of the day or early afternoon depending on the complexity of the case. It is difficult to ascertain how long a disciplinary hearing will take, so adequate time should be allowed. The disciplinary hearing should not be rushed; both parties should feel that they have their opportunity to state their case.

Essentially, the complaints against the employee and the evidence that has been gathered must be explained to the employee very clearly. The employee should then be allowed to set out and explain their case and answer the allegations. The employee should also be allowed to confer with their companion, dispute the evidence, ask questions, present their own evidence, explain any mitigating factors, call witnesses and be given a chance to raise points about information provided by witnesses. The employee (and companion) should be given the opportunity to question any witnesses if they disagree with the witness' evidence.

Once the facts have been established and both parties are satisfied that they have stated their case the disciplinary hearing should be adjourned in order for the chairperson to make their decision. It is quite normal and sometimes necessary for the disciplinary hearing to be adjourned until the next day – particularly when dismissal is being considered. There are usually factors that need to be considered that have come to light at the disciplinary hearing. This adjournment demonstrates that the chairperson will give the case due consideration and the outcome is not a foregone conclusion.

During the adjournment it is a good idea for the chairperson to write down the decision reached so that this forms part of the record of the meeting.

The disciplinary hearing should then be reconvened. All those present at the disciplinary hearing should attend apart from witnesses. The chair should explain the decision that they have made and the reasons for it – reading from the note written during the adjournment to avoid any misunderstandings. If a warning has been given, the employee should be told for how long this warning will be valid, what the standards of improvement are, the timescale for improvement and what support, if necessary, the employee will receive. They must also be advised that if their conduct or performance does not improve then further disciplinary action will be taken. Finally, they must also be advised of their right of appeal. A written letter confirming the outcome of the disciplinary hearing should be sent to the employee (see Appendix III: Letters E–K). This letter should not be written until after the disciplinary hearing has finished (in other words, after it has reconvened and after the chairperson has given the employee their decision) in order to avoid accusations that the decision was pre-judged, leading to claims of unfair dismissal.

THE DECISION

It must be clear to employees that the purpose of a fair disciplinary process is to ensure the chairperson comes to a reasonable decision based on the facts of the case. The chairperson is not required to prove the case against the employee *beyond all reasonable doubt*, as is the case for criminal cases, but they must be satisfied on the *balance of probabilities* that the employee acted as alleged. This means, that on the evidence available, having investigated the facts and heard the employee's explanation, it was more probable than not that the employee committed the alleged offence. Provided the chairperson is satisfied of this standard of proof any subsequent dismissal should be potentially fair.

When deciding whether a disciplinary penalty is appropriate, it is important to act reasonably in all the circumstances and bear in mind all relevant factors. The relevant factors include:

- The employee's general record, age, position and length of service.

- Whether the disciplinary procedure indicates what the likely penalty will be as a result of the particular misconduct.

- The extent to which standards have been breached.

- Any special circumstances such as provocation.

- Any mitigating factors for example, the employee's health or domestic situation.

- The gravity of the offence.

- The range of sanctions available within the disciplinary procedure.

- The likelihood of re-offending.

- Custom and practice – how has this situation been dealt with in the past in similar cases?

- Any *live* warnings on the employee's record?

- Is the decision reasonable in all the circumstances?

Where the facts of the case call for formal action, consider the following procedures:

STAGE 1 – FORMAL VERBAL WARNING
(SEE APPENDIX III: LETTER F)

Where, following a full investigation and disciplinary hearing, an employee is found guilty of a relatively minor offence (see Appendix I: 'Disciplinary Procedures' for examples), they should be given a formal verbal warning. This should set out the nature of the offence and the standard of behaviour or performance required. The employee should be advised that the warning is part of the formal disciplinary procedure and what the consequences will be of a failure to respond. This might be a first written warning, final written warning or ultimately dismissal. The employee should also be informed that they may appeal against the warning.

A record of the warning should be kept but normally disregarded after six months (the duration of warnings is set by the disciplinary procedure, not law, six months is typical). Note that time-expired warnings should not normally be a factor in deciding future disciplinary sanctions.

STAGE 2 – FIRST WRITTEN WARNING
(SEE APPENDIX III: LETTER G)

Where there is a failure to improve conduct or performance in the timescale set in the first warning, or where the matter is sufficiently serious (see Appendix I: 'Disciplinary Procedures' for examples), the employee may be given a first written warning. This should set out the nature of the offence and the change in behaviour or performance required. The employee should be advised that the warning is part of the formal disciplinary procedure and what the consequences will be of a failure to change. This might be a final written warning or ultimately dismissal. The employee should also be informed that they may appeal against the warning.

A record of the warning should be kept but disregarded after 12 months (or whatever time is in the Disciplinary Procedure). Note that the existence of time-expired warnings should not normally be a factor in deciding future disciplinary sanctions.

STAGE 3 – FINAL WRITTEN WARNING
(SEE APPENDIX III: LETTER H)

Where there is yet again a failure to improve conduct or performance in the timescale set, or where the conduct infringement is sufficiently serious (see Appendix I: 'Disciplinary Procedures' for examples), the employee may be given a final written warning. This should set out the nature of the offence and the change in behaviour or performance required. The employee should be advised that the warning is part of the formal disciplinary procedure and what the consequences will be of a failure to change. This might lead to either a dismissal or some other penalty. The employee should also be informed that they may appeal against the warning.

A record of the warning should be kept but disregarded after 12 months (or whatever time is in the Disciplinary Procedure). Note that the existence of time-expired warnings should not normally be a factor in deciding future disciplinary sanctions.

With warnings, a reasonable period of time should be allowed between each warning to allow the employee an opportunity to improve and for the manager to properly monitor the employee's conduct or performance. What is a reasonable time is not defined but will depend on the facts of the case and the type of misconduct or poor performance. For example, instances of insubordination may be met with a different stage of the disciplinary procedure on each occasion. A general complaint of poor performance or poor timekeeping will need to be monitored over a reasonable period of time to allow meaningful analysis of improvement or otherwise.

Managers should **not** progress to the next stage of the procedure where a substantially different type of offence has occurred – refer to Conduct or Capability section above. It would be unfair to issue a final written warning for poor performance if the employee is in receipt of a first written warning for a misconduct offence. The correct procedure would be to issue a formal verbal warning (or go through informal counselling) for the poor performance.

It must be remembered that before the next level of warning is given to an employee regardless of whether it is a repeat of the same or similar offence or whether performance has not improved, a full investigation must take place and a disciplinary hearing held in accordance with the company's disciplinary procedures.

OTHER SANCTIONS

For certain offences other sanctions may be appropriate to run alongside a formal warning. These might include the loss of a benefit (perhaps flexi-time or petrol allowance) through to loss of status, demotion, change of duties and so on – the latter only being appropriate for very serious offences as an alternative to dismissal. The company disciplinary procedure should include reference to other sanctions with some examples.

EXPIRED WARNINGS

After a period of time (typically six months for a formal verbal warning and 12 months for first and final written warnings), a warning will usually expire and should be disregarded for disciplinary purposes. The importance of a warning having lapsed is that in the event of further similar misconduct by the employee, the manager will have to go back to the preceding live relevant warning, if any, or start at the disciplinary stage relevant to the offence. To rely on an expired warning when dismissing an employee for a similar offence is likely to result in an unfair dismissal claim. However, if a similar offence has been committed shortly after the expiry of a warning, this can be taken into consideration, particularly where the offence is serious misconduct and the employee does not appear to have learned from the previous occasions.

The Data Protection Act does not require the employer to destroy disciplinary records altogether and there may be times when it is appropriate to retain these even well after expiry. They may be used to show (to a Tribunal perhaps) a pattern of warnings eventually leading to a dismissal. When defending personal injury claims, expired warnings may be a valuable source of evidence that protective equipment was issued and warnings given for non-compliance. Also in the event of a business takeover, the regulations (TUPE) indicate that any formal warnings issued in the preceding two years are disclosable to the potential buyer.

DISMISSAL WITH NOTICE
(SEE APPENDIX III: LETTER J)

Should similar misconduct or poor performance continue, the final stage is dismissal. Other penalties as an alternative to dismissal may be used instead; demotion, downgrading, salary penalty, changed duties, loss of seniority, compulsory training, relocation, or an extension to the final warning. Always consider whether the proposed outcome is reasonable in all the circumstances.

The decision to dismiss should only be taken by the chairperson of the disciplinary hearing and the employee should be informed as soon as possible of the reasons for dismissal, the appropriate period of notice, the date on which the contract of employment will terminate and the right of appeal. The decision to dismiss should be confirmed in writing (refer above to the six permitted reasons).

Unless the dismissal is on the grounds of gross misconduct, the employee must be given the appropriate period of notice to which he or she is entitled in law. Payment in lieu may be given for this notice period, if the contract allows for this. The Act lays down minimum notice periods, but these may be increased by the employee's contract of employment.

The **minimum statutory** notice periods are:

(a) one week for employees who have completed at least one month but less than two years' service (no notice entitlement if employed for under a month);

(b) thereafter one week for each completed year of service up to a maximum of 12 weeks, unless the contractual notice is greater.

The calculation of payment in lieu of notice should cover the value of any contractual benefits such as the use of a company car.

It should also be noted that if the dismissal is for sickness absence, normal payment should be made for the notice period, even where contractual sick pay has expired.

DISMISSAL WITHOUT NOTICE – GROSS MISCONDUCT
(SEE APPENDIX III: LETTER K)

Offences of gross misconduct usually warrant summary dismissal, in other words, dismissal without notice or payment for the notice period. However, *summary* dismissal is not the same as *instant* dismissal and incidents of gross misconduct will still need to be investigated and dealt with as part of a formal procedure. It is still important to establish the facts before taking any action. A short period of suspension may also be necessary (see 'Gross Misconduct – Suspension from Work' section above) pending the investigation.

Acts which constitute gross misconduct are those resulting in an extremely serious breach of contractual terms and should be detailed in the company disciplinary procedures. The gross misconduct act can either be an actual breach of an explicit term of the contract or a severe breakdown in the mutual trust and confidence that exists in every contract of employment. Fundamentally, the act is so severe that it goes to the heart of the contract and makes it impossible for the employment relationship to continue. Managers dealing with a gross misconduct case must consider these factors before dismissing for gross misconduct.

Note that although a gross misconduct dismissal means the employee loses the right to be paid their notice period, payment should still be made for any holiday untaken at the date of dismissal (statutory limit only, not the full contractual amount).

Employers must give all their employees a clear indication of the type of misconduct which will warrant dismissal without the normal period of notice being given. This is referred to as *summary dismissal* or is sometimes called *instant dismissal*. However, this latter description is dangerously misleading. Any instant dismissal is likely to be unfair as it implies that the proper procedures have not been followed.

Even where the case against the employee looks clear, the employee admits the offence or where an employee is caught red handed, a dismissal which takes place in breach of procedure, certainly without holding a full disciplinary hearing, is likely to be unfair. The word *summary dismissal* should be used and not the words *instant dismissal*.

APPEALS

Employees who have had formal disciplinary action taken against them should be given the opportunity to appeal. An employee may choose to appeal because they think a finding or penalty is unfair, new evidence has come to light or they think the disciplinary procedure was not followed correctly. It should be noted that the appeal stage is part of a best practice procedure and, is therefore, an essential part of any company disciplinary procedures.

The employee should put their appeal in writing within (typically) five working days of receipt of the decision, stating the reasons for the appeal. Note that if the employee states their intention to appeal, but does not put this in writing, it would still be advisable to make arrangements for the appeal to be heard. This should be sent to the chairperson of the disciplinary hearing. Normally appeals will be heard within 10 working days of the receipt of the employee's written notice.

It is important to know the grounds for the appeal so that an appropriate hearing is arranged. If the appeal is against the severity of the penalty, then a review of this decision is sufficient on appeal. The employee has perhaps admitted the offence but feels that the outcome is too harsh. This does not require all the witnesses to be involved again. However, if there is an appeal based on new evidence or a breach of procedure, it would be better to have a full new hearing with a different chair.

A Senior Manager/Director who has not been involved in the disciplinary procedure should hold the appeal hearing to make sure this can be decided entirely impartially. In certain situations, it has to be accepted that a more senior manager may not be available (perhaps in smaller organisations) to hear the appeal. In these circumstances, it will be acceptable for another manager of the same status to deal with the appeal. However, it must be stressed that whoever deals with an appeal against a disciplinary sanction must not have been involved in the initial decision. As before, the employee has the right to be accompanied by a fellow employee or a trade union representative and a letter notifying them of an appeal hearing should be sent to the employee (see Appendix III: Letter L).

At the appeal hearing, the chairperson should explain the reasons for the appeal hearing and invite the employee or their companion to present the appeal. The chairperson should listen to the facts of the appeal and consider new evidence as appropriate. It may be appropriate and reasonable for the appeal to adjourn whilst the chairperson investigates the facts of the appeal and to reconvene once this has been completed. As with a disciplinary hearing, timing is crucial and this must concluded without delay.

In any event the appeal hearing should adjourn before any decision is made. The chairperson will need to make a decision on the outcome, based on the facts raised at the appeal hearing, confirming that the original disciplinary decision is either upheld, withdrawn, will be reviewed or replaced by another sanction. The outcome must be communicated to the employee when the appeal hearing is reconvened and later confirmed in writing (see Appendix III: Letter M). This is the normally the final stage of the disciplinary procedure, but some organisations offer further levels of appeal in their procedures, so always check the Discipline Policy. There is no legal obligation to offer more than one appeal, and this is the recommended position.

Some businesses have the option in the policy to increase the sanction on appeal. It is felt that this option discourages those employees who appeal without justification. Whilst again this is perfectly lawful it needs to be used sparingly and only for very good reasons. If however, new evidence comes to light during the appeal stage – which could lead to the penalty being increased, it is recommended that the employer goes back a stage and writes a letter to the employee containing the new allegations – effectively holding a new disciplinary hearing.

If the appeal is made following a decision to dismiss the employee – it is important to clarify the actual date of termination. This will determine the employment status of the employee during the appeals process. If an individual is summarily dismissed, following a hearing, for gross misconduct – an appeal must be offered. If the employee does appeal, this does not reverse the dismissal decision. Effectively they will remain an ex-employee during the appeals process. The decision made at the appeal will in effect determine the outcome. If the appeal decision confirms the dismissal, the date of termination will be the original date, not the date of the appeal.

CRIMINAL OFFENCES AND PROCEEDINGS

There may be occasions when an employee commits a criminal offence or is involved in a serious incident away from the work place and out of work time. These should not be treated as automatic reasons for dismissal. The manager must have due regard to whether the offence or incident has any relevance to the duties of the individual as an employee. The main considerations should be whether the act is one that has undermined the mutual trust and confidence between the parties or makes the employee unsuitable for their type of work or unacceptable to other employees. If this is the case then the company disciplinary procedure should be followed.

Where it is alleged the employee has committed a criminal act, inside or outside the work place that potentially affects the employee's employment and the police are proceeding with their own investigations, this can impede the internal disciplinary hearing. In such circumstances, it is rarely acceptable for the manager to do nothing until the outcome of the criminal investigation. The manager should attempt to come to a decision as to the employee's guilt and whether, if at all, this affects the employment relationship. This requires a hearing to be held and decision to be made. If the decision is to dismiss the employee and this is implemented and then the employee is acquitted of the criminal charge, the dismissal will not necessarily be unfair. Fairness will depend on the procedure adopted and the facts available to the manager at the time of the decision. Remember, the burden of proof for dismissal is 'on the balance of probability'.

RECORDS AND DATA PROTECTION

The company is obliged keep records detailing the nature of any breach of disciplinary rules, the employee's defence or mitigation, the action taken and the reasons for it. Details of appeals, where lodged by the employee, should also be kept. The company should keep these records safely and confidentially and retain them in accordance with the Data Protection Act, which requires the release of certain data to individuals on their request (see below). Copies of disciplinary hearing records, including copies of the formal minutes taken, should be given to the employee concerned.

Under data protection law, employees have the right, on written request, to receive a copy of their personnel files (provided they form part of a relevant filing system) and any computer data held on them, and to demand that any inaccuracies be corrected or removed. The Data Protection Act contains eight basic principles to be complied in connection with the processing of personal data.

Employees are entitled on written request:

- To be told by the company whether personal data about them is being processed.

- To be given a description of the data concerned; the purposes for which it is being processed, and the recipients or classes of recipients to whom it is or may be disclosed.

- To have communicated in an intelligible form the personal data concerned and any information available to the Company as to the source of the data.

- To be informed in certain circumstances of the logic involved in computerised decision-making.

The company is not obliged to supply the information mentioned above unless the employee has made a written request and the employer may levy a fee, up to a maximum (at the time of writing this was set at £10). The company must comply with the request within 40 days.

Where the company fails to correct inaccurate data, an employee has the right to apply to the court (not a tribunal) on the grounds that the personal data relating to them is inaccurate. If the complaint is upheld, the court may order the employer to rectify, block, erase or destroy that data and any other personal data containing an expression of opinion based on the inaccurate information. If the inaccurate data has been disclosed to third parties, the court may also order the company to notify those third parties that the inaccurate information has been corrected.

SUMMARY DISMISSAL AND HOLIDAY PAY

A summary dismissal takes place where the employee has committed gross misconduct. In these circumstances, employers often refuse to pay outstanding holiday pay as the employee's conduct has been so bad that it amounts to a breach of contract, and they lose their holiday pay.

However, the Working Time Regulations state that an employee will be entitled to a payment for untaken holiday, which exists at the termination of employment. The regulations do not mention summary dismissal for gross misconduct.

Managers should therefore make a note that it is a breach of the Working Time Regulations to fail to pay accrued holiday pay to an employee who is dismissed for gross misconduct. It should be noted however, that this only applies to the statutory holiday rights found in the Working Time Regulations. Any contractual holiday pay over and above the statutory could be withheld in the event of a summary dismissal for gross misconduct.

CONSTRUCTIVE DISMISSAL

This is not actually a dismissal by the employer. An employee resigns, or simply leaves, as a result of their treatment by the employer.

Constructive dismissal involves a situation where the individual worker feels they have no alternative but to leave their work because of their employer's conduct.

The employee must demonstrate that they resigned as a direct result of a serious or fundamental breach of the employment contract by their employer. As a result of ACAS guidance the employee will normally be expected to put their grievance in writing to the employer, and give the employer a chance to respond, before a tribunal will accept their complaint.

STATUTORY GUIDELINES

Discipline is an issue that attracts regulation and from time to time certain statutory requirements are imposed on businesses.

In 2004, Statutory Disciplinary Procedures were introduced but attracted criticism immediately from all sides due to the over-formal structure they involved. These are being withdrawn and replaced with an updated Code of Practice to be drawn up by ACAS. The guidelines contained in this manual reflect best practice at the time of writing (2008) and should not be affected by changes in legislation in the foreseeable future. However, particularly when contemplating dismissal, do check for the latest position by visiting the ACAS website and reviewing the latest Code of Practice (www.acas.org.uk).

APPENDIX I

Model Company Disciplinary Procedure (Conduct)

The Purpose of the Procedures

The purpose of the company's disciplinary rules and procedures is to help all employees to achieve and maintain acceptable standards of conduct, attendance and job performance. The company recognises that disciplinary action should not be viewed solely as a means of imposing sanctions but rather as a means of encouraging improvement. These rules and procedures are company policy statements, do not form part of your contract of employment and are for information purposes only.

These procedures do not apply to staff during their probationary period.

Poor performance resulting from lack of skill, qualification, ability, competence, or effort despite having received usual levels of training and support should be handled under the Capability Procedure.

Principles

All cases of formal disciplinary action under these procedures will be recorded and placed with the company's records. At every stage in the formal procedure you will be advised in writing of the nature of the complaint against you and be given the opportunity to state your case before any decision is made. You will have the right to be accompanied by a trade union representative or a work-based colleague of your choosing. You will have the right to appeal against any formal disciplinary sanctions.

In operating this policy, managers will apply the organisation's commitment to equality by treating all employees fairly and without discrimination on the grounds of colour, race, ethnic or national origins, sexual orientation, age, marital status, disability, trade union association or religious beliefs.

An employee who is subject to discipline should not normally be considered for promotion, although a sideways move, or work at a lower grade should not be ruled out if it is felt to be appropriate and would result in improved performance.

Informal Counselling

Informal counselling may be a more appropriate response to minor offences rather than formal disciplinary action. If appropriate, counselling will take the form of a discussion with the object of determining and agreeing the improvement required. Where this informal approach fails to bring about the desired improvement, (or the offence is of a more serious nature) the formal procedure will then be followed. A file note may be made by the manager of this informal meeting.

Investigations

No action will be taken by the company before a proper investigation has been undertaken. If appropriate the company may suspend you from work for a specified period during which time such an investigation will be undertaken. You will initially be paid your normal salary and benefits during any suspension. During the period of suspension, however, you will not be entitled to access to the company's premises, except with the prior consent of the company and subject to such conditions as the company may impose. You are expected to be contactable during normal working hours should the need arise to speak to you. Any breach of these conditions will entitle the company to consider making the suspension unpaid.

Disciplinary Hearing

If, under these procedures, the company decides to hold a disciplinary hearing in relation to the matter complained of, you will be given written details of the complaint against you at least three working days before any disciplinary hearing takes place.

If, for good cause, the employee is unable to attend the hearing, it will be adjourned to another date convenient to both parties and depending upon the circumstances. If the employee is unable to attend the rearranged hearing it will proceed in his or her absence unless there are overriding reasons why it should not. The representative may present the case on the employee's behalf and any written submissions from the employee will be considered.

At any disciplinary hearing you will be given an opportunity to state your case. Offences under the company's disciplinary procedures fall into two main categories:

(a) misconduct/gross misconduct;
(b) poor performance, sickness absence.

The following sanction may be applied as a result of a disciplinary hearing:

STAGE 1 – FORMAL VERBAL WARNING

If conduct or performance is unsatisfactory, you will be given a formal verbal warning which will be recorded and will normally last for a period of six months but, subject to satisfactory conduct or performance, will be disregarded following the expiry of that period.

STAGE 2 – FIRST WRITTEN WARNING

If the offence is of a more serious nature or if, following a verbal warning, your conduct or performance is still unsatisfactory, a first written warning will be given to you which will state the reason for the warning and will require an improvement in your conduct or performance within a stipulated time period, failing which further disciplinary action will be taken. The written warning will normally last for a period of 12 months but, subject to satisfactory conduct and performance, will be disregarded following the expiry of that period.

STAGE 3 – FINAL WRITTEN WARNING

If the offence is very serious but does not amount to gross misconduct or if, following a first written warning, your conduct or performance is still unsatisfactory, a final written warning will be given which will state the reason for the warning and will require an improvement in your conduct or performance, failing which further disciplinary action will result which could ultimately lead to dismissal. This warning will normally last for a period of 12 months but, subject to satisfactory conduct or performance, will be disregarded following the expiry of that period.

STAGE 4 – DISMISSAL

If, following a final written warning there is no satisfactory improvement in your conduct or performance within the specified time period, you will be subject to further disciplinary action which could lead to you being dismissed.

The company reserves the right to make a payment in lieu of notice on the termination of your contract, other than in cases of gross misconduct.

These warnings are normally issued in sequence, however in cases of serious or gross misconduct or where there is a pattern of persistent poor performance or misconduct, the sequence of warnings outlined above may not be followed. The procedure may be instigated at any stage felt appropriate by the company.

Note: In addition to the disciplinary warnings outlined above, in cases of serious or gross misconduct further disciplinary measures may be invoked. These alternative measures include: a transfer to another job or location, demotion to a lower grade, withdrawal of flexible working privileges, reduction in sick pay entitlement or deductions from salary to cover repayment for loss or damage to company property.

Misconduct

Examples of misconduct are:

(a) bad time keeping;
(b) unreasonable or unexplained absence;
(c) persistent absenteeism;
(d) minor damage to the Company's property;
(e) smoking in no-smoking areas;
(f) misuse of Company property;
(g) non-submission of medical certificate or breach of sickness notification procedure;
(h) use of obscene or offensive language;
(i) breach of health and safety rules.

This list contains examples only and is not intended to be exhaustive.

Gross Misconduct

Examples of gross misconduct are:

(a) theft;
(b) physical assault;
(c) gross insubordination;
(d) abusive behaviour;
(e) breach of duty of confidentiality;
(f) sexual, racial or disability harassment, bullying or other breaches of the company Equal Opportunity Policy, including Age discrimination;
(g) fighting on the premises;
(h) vandalism or wilful damage to Company property;
(i) serious breach of health and safety rules or procedures;
(j) making false or fraudulent claims against the Company – falsification of records, expenses claims, time recording;
(k) sale and/or consumption of alcohol or drugs on Company premises or being under the influence of alcohol or drugs at work;
(l) failure to comply with lawful and reasonable instructions;
(m) bringing the Company's name into disrepute;
(n) abuse of e-mail or Internet access.

This list contains examples only and is not intended to be exhaustive.

If it is established, after investigation and after hearing your explanation of the matter, that you have committed an act of gross misconduct you will be summarily dismissed, in other words, without notice and/or any pay in lieu thereof. While the alleged gross misconduct is being investigated you may be suspended (on full pay) in accordance with the provision set out above. If the company takes the decision to dismiss you, you will be advised of the reason for the dismissal and the date upon which your employment will be terminated.

Appeals

If you wish to appeal against any disciplinary decision taken by the company at any stage, you may do so, in the first instance, by appealing to (appropriate name(s) or job title(s)) within five working days of the disciplinary decision being received by you. You should state the reason for your appeal. At such appeal you will be entitled to attend to state your case and to be accompanied by an employee of the company of your choice or by a representative of any recognised union of which you are a member. The decision of (appropriate name(s) or job title(s)) will be final.

APPENDIX II

Model Capability Performance Improvement Procedure

Purpose of Procedure

The aim of this Procedure is to help staff to improve under-performance at an early stage for the benefit of the individual, the team and the business. Good leadership is about taking early action when they identify a member of the team is not performing.

These procedures do not apply to staff during their probationary period, and do not form part of your contract of employment.

Relationship with the Staff Appraisal System

This procedure has been separated from the appraisal process to allow prompt and speedy action to be taken, and to clarify that the processes required are different. Managers who are concerned about poor performance must not wait until the formal appraisal review is due.

Points to Consider

Line managers should explore possible causes of poor performance with the employee so that the problem is properly understood before discussing remedial action. Otherwise the action agreed may not be appropriate. This checklist of issues to consider may be helpful:

- An underlying health problem.

- Personal or domestic issues affecting performance.

- Lack of experience, training or qualification to do the job. Has proper and sufficient training been given?

- Reorganisation of work or redistribution of duties if this will help. Perhaps on a temporary basis initially.

- Has there been a recent change in the person's line management responsibilities or in the reporting line?

- Has there been a recent change in the work role or duties?

- Has there been a gradual deterioration in standards, or has it happened suddenly? If so explore why.

- Is performance always poor or are there times when it is better than others?

- Are some tasks/types of works performed better than others?

Poor Performance or Misconduct?

This process runs in parallel with, but is not part of, the Company Disciplinary (Misconduct) Procedure. Poor performance resulting from lack of skill, qualification, ability, competence, or effort despite having received usual levels of training and support should be handled under this process. However a pattern of wilful inappropriate behaviour, careless mistakes or serious negligence leading to or resulting in loss, damage or other negative consequences for the business may be treated as misconduct. If in doubt, please seek advice about the appropriate approach.

The company expects all staff to be able to perform their duties and demonstrate appropriate competencies to an acceptable level for their job role and pay band. Poor performance occurs when any aspect of performance or competence drops to an unsatisfactory level for the individual's grade (even if the poor performance is only a small element of their job). In these circumstances line managers should follow the following guidance.

Informal Guidance

Before starting formal Stage 1 of this process (see below), managers must take preliminary remedial action to deal with any shortcomings as soon as they become apparent. Addressing the issue promptly will increase the likelihood of resolving it successfully. This is an informal stage of the process; but there may be operational consequences (see below).

Preliminary remedial action requires meetings with the under-performing employee and may involve: giving further feedback, coaching, advice and support, additional training.

The aim throughout is to help the employee to reach an acceptable standard of performance. However, it should be made clear that if the individual cannot meet the required standard of performance, within a certain timeframe (probably no more than 12 weeks depending on circumstances) specified by the manager, then formal Stage 1 of the process will start.

If an employee is receiving informal guidance when their appraisal falls due, completion of the appraisal can be delayed.

An employee who is subject to informal guidance should not normally be considered for promotion, although a sideways move, or work at a lower grade should not be ruled out if it is felt to be appropriate and would result in improved performance.

Informal meetings should normally be one to one discussions. The employee is not entitled to a companion at this point, as no sanctions can be applied by the manager in this part of the process.

When the employee responds successfully to informal guidance this should be acknowledged by the manager. However, the manager should inform the employee that should performance return to an unsatisfactory level for the same reasons within the next 12 months, the formal stages will be commenced – there will not be a further informal guidance stage.

Formal Performance/Capability Process

OVERVIEW OF KEY STAGES

- Stage 1 – First Formal Warning and Monitoring

- Stage 2 – Final Warning and Final Monitoring

- Stage 3 – Dismissal or Other Appropriate Action

STAGE 1 – FIRST FORMAL WARNING AND MONITORING

Stage 1 starts if informal guidance has failed to produce an improvement in performance to an agreed standard. The line manager should hold an interview with the employee and cover the following:

- Clarify that this is a Stage 1 warning situation. Give the employee a copy of the formal procedure; provide examples of under-performance and say specifically what needs to change.

- Explain what support or training will be given.

- Set a monitoring period for improvement (usually three to six months).

- Set dates or timescales for regularly monitoring and reviewing progress.

- State the possible outcomes of the monitoring period.

When arranging the interview the line manager should:

- Inform the employee in writing that he/she is required to attend an interview and set out in broad terms the areas of performance that need to improve.

- Give the employee a minimum of three working days notice (be flexible to accommodate accompaniment by trade union official).

- Advise the employee that they may bring a trade union official or a current work colleague to the interview if they wish. (Cost of any travel will not be met by the business).

The accompanying person should be allowed to participate during the meeting (for example, making a statement at the start and/or finish of the meeting to present the employee's case and to sum up and to respond to views/ask questions; request a break to confer and so on). The companion cannot speak for the employee however. The line manager may ask an HR manager or another colleague senior to the employee to act as a note-taker.

At the end of the interview, the line manager should:

- Record the key points of the discussion and warning (provided the manager is satisfied that a warning is still justified) in writing. If possible, agree the text with the employee to ensure their views are accurately reflected. It is important to state the area of under-performance explicitly and in most cases give two or three examples; the level of performance expected should also be spelt out as clearly as possible (standards).

- Give a copy of the record to the employee along with the letter with an additional copy of both, which he/she should be asked to sign within a week.

   (if the employee refuses to sign the record this fact should be noted on the record by the line manager)

- Retain a copy of the letter and any additional notes made.

- Advise the employee of their right of appeal.

- Set a date for the first formal monitoring/review of progress.

- Ensure that all reasonable help and support is given during the monitoring period.

If unsure what help is appropriate, seek advice.

Stage 1 – First Formal Warning – Appeals Procedure

If an employee challenges the basis of the warning, he/she may appeal in writing to (name of appropriate manager or director)

On receipt of the appeal:

- (Name of appropriate manager or director) should discuss the case with the line manager and an HR manager and then interview the employee. The employee has the right to a personal hearing and to be accompanied by a TU Representative or current work colleague.

- (Name of appropriate manager or director) will then decide if the Stage 1 warning should stand. This decision will be final.

- The employee will be advised of the outcome of the appeal in writing normally within three days of the appeal being heard.

- If the appeal is unsuccessful, the first monitoring period will begin from the date the employee is informed of the outcome.

Stage 1 – Possible Outcomes Following the First Monitoring Period

At the end of the first monitoring period, the outcome will be one of the following:

i) *Performance has improved to the required standard*

Tell the employee that, if they continue to work at the required standard, no further action will be taken. Advise that if, within a period of one year from the date of the letter, they cease to maintain the required standard, the performance/capability process will be reinstated at Formal Stage 2.

ii) *Performance has not improved (and been maintained) to the required standard*

Proceed to Stage 2 below, unless the line manager acknowledges that not enough has been done to help the individual to improve. In these cases it may be appropriate to repeat the Stage 1 warning. This might also be appropriate in exceptional circumstances where there are other genuine mitigating factors (for example, sudden illness, disability, bereavement and so on). If this is being considered, advice must be sought from the HR manager.

Formal Stage 2 – Final Warning and Final Monitoring Period

The Stage 2 interview should follow the same process as outlined for Stage 1 above. However, it must be made clear to the employee that this constitutes a <u>final</u> warning under Stage 2 of the procedure, and that unsatisfactory completion of the final monitoring period is very likely to result in dismissal, transfer or downgrading.

STAGE 2 – APPEALS

If the employee challenges the reasons for the issue of a Stage 2 warning, he/she may appeal in writing to (name of appropriate manager or director) within five days of receiving the written warning.

The employee and their manager will be advised of the outcome of the appeal in writing, normally within three days of the appeal being heard. If the appeal is unsuccessful the final monitoring period will begin from the date the employee is informed of the outcome.

STAGE 2 – POSSIBLE OUTCOMES FOLLOWING FINAL WARNING AND FINAL MONITORING

At the end of the final monitoring period, the outcome will be one of the following:

i) Performance has improved to the required standard

Tell the employee that, whilst the required standard of performance is sustained, no further action will arise. Confirm in writing.

Advise that if, within a period of one year from the date of the letter, the employee ceases to perform to the required standard, action will automatically be taken against them under Stage 3 of the procedure.

ii) Performance has not improved to the required standard

Proceed to Stage 3 below, unless the line manager acknowledges that not enough has been done to help the employee to improve. In these cases it may be appropriate to repeat the Stage 2 warning. It might also be appropriate in exceptional circumstances where there are other genuine mitigating factors (for example, sudden illness, disability, bereavement and so on). If this is being considered, approval must be sought from the HR manager. Notify the employee of your decision.

Stage 3 – Dismissal or Other Appropriate Action

If the line manager and departmental manager agree that the employee's performance has not sufficiently improved following the Stage 2 final warning and final monitoring period, the employee's case should be submitted to the HR manager for a decision on dismissal, transfer or downgrading.

STAGE 3 – TRANSFER TO OTHER WORK

Following unsuccessful completion of any formal monitoring period, the line manager should consider whether the employee should continue with his or her present duties or be transferred to other work. Whatever decision is made the employee must remain on the capability procedure.

If transfer is considered, it should be discussed with the employee and the effect on him/her should be included in decision-making. The HR manager should approve requests for transfer. The HR manager will be responsible for taking action to effect the move.

STAGE 3 – APPEALS

If the employee wishes to appeal against the decision he/she may do so in writing, within seven working days of hearing the decision, to the HR director.

APPENDIX III

Letter A

Suspension from Work

(Date)

(Name)
(Address)

Dear *(Name)*

**PRECAUTIONARY SUSPENSION FROM WORK
(ALTERNATIVELY: TEMPORARY RELIEF FROM DUTY)**

Further to our meeting yesterday afternoon, this letter formally confirms that you are suspended from duty, on full pay, under the company's disciplinary procedure pending investigations into *(details of the serious/gross misconduct.)* *(Name and title)* was also present at this meeting.

In accordance with the company's Disciplinary Procedure, I have considered whether this is a necessary step in the circumstances of the case. Following consideration of alternatives to suspension, I have concluded that this is the most appropriate action at this time, subject to on-going reviews. It does not mean that you have been, or will be found guilty of any particular offence or act of misconduct.

The suspension is initially with full pay and you remain in employment with the company. You should, therefore, be available to attend meetings as required within your normal working hours. I must point out that any failure to attend without good reason, and any other breach of the terms of this suspension, will lead to a possible move to suspension without pay, and further disciplinary action.

You will be informed of the outcome of the investigation as soon as possible, and if no disciplinary action is needed you will also be informed which date to resume work. If the outcome of the investigation requires you to attend a disciplinary hearing, then you will be informed of the date and time of the hearing.

Whilst suspended you must refrain from entering onto company property and must not make contact with any member of the company's staff (*if appropriate, add: or clients and customers*) without permission from myself. Should this investigation lead to a disciplinary hearing, you will be provided with access to any staff or other information at your workplace for the purposes of preparing your case.

We do appreciate that suspension is a serious step to take and we will make every effort to investigate this alleged (misconduct) fairly and promptly. Your suspension from duty is part of that process, and does not imply in any way that you have committed this offence.

If you have any questions in relation to this suspension or your position, you should contact me in the first instance.

Yours sincerely,

(Name)
Director

APPENDIX III

Letter B

Notification of an Investigatory Meeting

(Date)

(Name)
(Address)

Dear *(Name)*

NOTIFICATION OF AN INVESTIGATORY MEETING

I am writing to ask you to attend an investigatory meeting on *(date)* at *(time)* at *(location)*. This meeting has been arranged because I am in the process of investigating allegations that have been made relating to your *(details of the conduct/performance)*.

Please note that the purpose of the meeting is entirely a fact-finding exercise, and is not a disciplinary hearing. If, once the investigation has been concluded, it is decided to institute disciplinary proceedings against you; you will be invited to attend a formal disciplinary hearing at a later date.

The investigatory meeting will be conducted by *(name/s)* and *(name)* will also be present to take notes of the meeting.

If you are unable to attend this meeting, you are asked to contact me as a matter of urgency so that an alternative date and time can be scheduled. I would advise you that it is in your interests to attend the meeting so that you can give your account of events before a decision is taken by me on whether or not to proceed to a disciplinary hearing. If you fail to attend without good reason, a decision on the institution of disciplinary proceedings will be made in your absence and may also result in any further period of suspension being without pay.

Once I have completed the investigation, you will be informed of the outcome.

Yours sincerely,

(Name)
Line Manager

NOTE: Strictly speaking this type of meeting does not attract the legal right to a companion. However, if the company disciplinary procedure allows this, or if in the circumstances you feel it to be appropriate – when dealing with an employee with a disability, or a young worker for example – consider adding that a work colleague or trade union official can also attend.

APPENDIX III

Letter C

Confirmation of No Action Following an Investigatory Meeting

(Date)

(Name)
(Address)

Dear *(Name)*

OUTCOME OF THE DISCIPLINARY INVESTIGATION

Further to the recent investigation into your alleged (*details of alleged performance or misconduct*), it has been decided that no formal disciplinary action will be taken against you on this occasion.

(If appropriate, add:) However, under the circumstances it has been decided to arrange informal *coaching/counselling/training* to address the issues we discussed. *(Provide details here).*

Thank you for cooperating in this investigation.

Yours sincerely,

(Name)
Line Manager

APPENDIX III

Letter D

Notification of a Disciplinary Hearing

(Date)

(Name)
(Address)

Dear *(Name)*

NOTIFICATION OF A DISCIPLINARY HEARING

I write to inform you that you are required to attend a formal Disciplinary Hearing to be held on *(date)* at *(time)* at *(location)* to consider whether disciplinary action should be taken against you. *(Allow a minimum of 2 working days before holding the meeting, possibly longer if the offence could result in dismissal)* This gives you a reasonable opportunity to consider your response to the company's position.

The background facts and evidence are attached for your information.

A full investigation of the facts surrounding the complaint(s) against you has now been made. Having now completed that investigation, the allegations against you are as follows:

- *(List each of the allegations in full detail, sticking to the facts and taking care over the wording to avoid implying guilt and avoid using accusatory words like 'stolen', 'falsified' or similar).*

(Where discipline is for potential gross misconduct, add:) In the company's view and in accordance with the Disciplinary Procedure, these allegations constitute gross misconduct offences and therefore could lead to action up to and including your summary dismissal.

For your information, copies of the following documents are enclosed by way of evidence:

- *(Provide copies of all witness statements – which should be signed and dated – and any other supporting documentary evidence that you intend to produce and rely on at the disciplinary hearing. Consider adding a copy of the company discipline procedure).*

These documents form the basis for the company's complaint(s) and the company will therefore rely on these documents in support of the allegations made against you.

If you would like to submit a written statement for consideration in advance of the hearing you may do so. This should be forwarded to me.

At the hearing, you will of course be given a full opportunity to explain your case and answer the allegations. You may ask questions, dispute the evidence, provide your own evidence, call witnesses and otherwise argue your case. You may also put forward any mitigating factors which you consider relevant to your case. Due consideration will be given to any factors or explanations which you raise when considering what, if any, disciplinary sanctions are to be imposed. Please let me know in advance if you intend to call any witnesses. You should make arrangements for any witnesses in support of your case to attend the Hearing. Alternatively you may wish to produce statements from witnesses and if so you should bring these to the meeting. If you would like any assistance in organising this do let me know.

The disciplinary hearing will be chaired by *(name)* and *(name)* will also be present to take notes of the hearing.

You have the right to be accompanied at the disciplinary hearing. Your companion may be either a fellow employee or a trade union representative of your choice. Your companion will be permitted to address the hearing and to confer with you during the hearing but they will not be permitted to answer questions on your behalf. Please inform me in advance of the identity of your chosen companion. *(If the employee has a disability or language difficulty, or they are a young worker do consider allowing an appropriate companion to provide support – they may be from outside the business)*

(Where the employee already has a related, active final written warning on file, add:) Since you already have a related, active final written warning on your personnel file, I must inform you that the outcome of this disciplinary hearing could result in your dismissal from employment.

If you or your chosen companion is unable to attend this disciplinary hearing, you are asked to contact me as a matter of urgency so that an alternative date and time can be scheduled. *(Employees have the right to request up to a five-day delay in the date of this meeting if their choice of companion is not available)* You are reminded that you are required to take all reasonable steps to attend the hearing. Failure to attend without good reason could result in the hearing being held, and a decision being taken, in your absence. However, if you fail to attend through circumstances completely outside your control and which are currently unforeseeable, the company will arrange another hearing. Thereafter, if you fail to attend for a second time without good reason, the hearing will be held, and a decision will be taken, in your absence.

At the end of the disciplinary hearing, you will be informed in writing of the company's decision, and in accordance with the disciplinary procedure you will be offered the chance to appeal.

Further to my letter to you dated *(date)* you will remain on suspension with full pay until the date of the disciplinary hearing.

Yours sincerely,

(Name)
Manager

APPENDIX III

Letter E

Confirmation of No Action Following a Disciplinary Hearing

(Date)

(Name)
(Address)

Dear *(Name)*

OUTCOME OF THE DISCIPLINARY HEARING

Further to your disciplinary hearing which was conducted by me on *(date)*, it has been decided that no formal disciplinary action will be taken against you on this occasion.

Thank you for your co-operation in this matter

Yours sincerely,

(Name)
Line Manager

APPENDIX III

Letter F

Formal Stage 1 – Verbal Warning

(Date)

(Name)
(Address)

Dear *(Name)*

FORMAL STAGE 1 (VERBAL) WARNING

Further to your disciplinary hearing which was conducted by *(name)*, held on *(date)* regarding *(details of incident),* this letter constitutes confirmation of a formal stage 1 (verbal) warning. A copy of this letter will be placed on your personnel file, and will remain active for 6 months.

At the hearing you were given the right to be accompanied and you chose to *waive this right/have in attendance (name).*

As you know, a full investigation of the facts surrounding the complaint against you was made. Having put the specific facts to you for your comment at the disciplinary hearing, it was decided that your explanation was not acceptable in the circumstances. For this reason, it was deemed appropriate to warn you formally in writing about the following aspects of your conduct/performance which are, in the company's view, unacceptable:

- *(List each of the complaints giving rise to the warning).*

You now need to improve your conduct/performance in the following ways:

- *(List how the employee needs to improve their conduct, behaviour, or work performance in relation to each of the complaints. This needs to be specific with targets if appropriate and time scales for the improvement. Vague wording such as 'you must improve your attendance' are not sufficient).*

This formal verbal warning forms part of the formal disciplinary process and will remain active for a period of 6 months from *(date of letter)*. It will therefore expire on *(date)*. If within that time period there is further cause for dissatisfaction in respect of similar misconduct/poor performance to that described above, more serious disciplinary action may be taken against you. The consequences could be a written warning, a final written warning and, ultimately, dismissal. It is hoped that this warning will lead to an immediate, substantial and sustained level of improvement in your conduct so that such action will not be necessary.

This letter will be placed on your personal file for the duration of the warning. When the warning has expired it will then be removed from your file. In accordance with our data protection policy, the human resources department will keep a record of this warning.

You have the right to appeal against this decision if you are not satisfied with it. If you do wish to appeal, you must inform the company in writing of the reason for your appeal, within *(X)* days, in accordance with the company's disciplinary procedure, a copy of which is attached for your information. If you do appeal, the company will then invite you to attend an appeal hearing.

Yours sincerely,

(Name)
Line Manager

Please sign and return a copy of this formal verbal warning letter to indicate that you have received it and understand its contents.

Signed: ....   Date:

....
    (Name of employee)

APPENDIX III

Letter G

Formal Stage 2 – First Written Warning

(Date)

(Name)
(Address)

Dear *(Name)*

STAGE 2 (FIRST WRITTEN) WARNING

Further to your disciplinary hearing which was conducted by *(name)*, held on *(date)* regarding *(details of incident)*, this letter constitutes confirmation of a stage 2 (first written) warning. A copy of this letter will be placed on your personnel file and will remain active for 12 months.

At the hearing you were given the right to be accompanied and you chose to *waive this right/have in attendance (name)*.

As you know, a full investigation of the facts surrounding the complaint against you was made. Having put the specific facts to you for your comment at the disciplinary hearing, it was decided that your explanation was not acceptable in the circumstances. For this reason, *(if appropriate, add:)* and in consideration of a previous active first stage (verbal) warning you received for similar performance/misconduct it was deemed appropriate to issue you with a formal written warning (stage 2) about the following aspects of your conduct/capability which are, in the company's view, unacceptable:

- *(List each of the complaints giving rise to the warning)*.

You now need to improve your performance/conduct in the following ways:

- *(List how the employee needs to improve their performance or conduct in relation to each of the complaints. This needs to be specific with targets if appropriate and time scales for the improvement. Vague wording such as 'you must improve your attendance or performance' are not sufficient).*

This first written warning forms part of the formal disciplinary process and will remain active for a period of 12 months from *(date of letter)*. It will therefore expire on *(date)*. If within that time period there is further cause for dissatisfaction in respect of similar misconduct/poor performance to that described above, more serious disciplinary action may be taken against you. The consequences could be a final written warning and, ultimately, dismissal. It is hoped that this warning will lead to an immediate, substantial and sustained level of improvement in your conduct/performance so that further such action will not be necessary. *(If relevant, add:)* Please note that this first written warning has been issued to you as the first stage of the company's disciplinary procedure given the seriousness of your conduct.

This letter will be placed on your personal file for the duration of the warning. When the warning has expired it will then be removed from your file. In accordance with our data protection policy, the human resources department will keep a record of this warning.

You have the right to appeal against this decision if you are not satisfied with it. If you do wish to appeal, you must inform the company in writing of the reason for your appeal within *(X)* days, in accordance with the company's disciplinary procedure, a copy of which is attached for your information. If you do appeal, the company will then invite you to attend an appeal hearing which you must take all reasonable steps to attend.

Yours sincerely,

(Name)
Line Manager

Please sign and return a copy of this first written warning letter to indicate that you have received it and understand its contents.

Signed: ....   Date:

....
(Name of employee)

APPENDIX III

Letter H

Formal Stage 3 – Final Written Warning

(Date)

(Name)
(Address)

Dear *(Name)*

FINAL WRITTEN WARNING

Further to your disciplinary hearing which was conducted by *(name)*, held on *(date)* regarding *(details of incident)*, this letter constitutes confirmation of a final written warning. A copy of this letter will be placed on your personnel file and will remain active for 12 months.

At the hearing you were given the right to be accompanied and you chose to *waive this right/have in attendance (name)*.

As you know, a full investigation of the facts surrounding the complaint against you was made. Having put the specific facts to you for your comment at the disciplinary hearing, it was decided that your explanation was not acceptable in the circumstances. For this reason, *(if appropriate, add:)* and in consideration of a previous active first written warning you received for similar performance/ misconduct, it was deemed appropriate to formally issue a final warning (stage 3) to you in writing about the following aspects of your conduct/performance which are, in the company's view, unacceptable:

- *(List each of the complaints giving rise to the warning).*

You now need to improve your conduct/performance in the following ways:

- *(List how the employee needs to improve their conduct/ performance in relation to each of the complaints. This needs to be specific with targets if appropriate and time scales for the improvement. Vague wording such as 'you must improve your attendance' are not sufficient).*

This final written warning forms part of the formal disciplinary process and will remain active for a period of 12 months from *(date of letter)*. It will therefore expire on *(date)*. If within that time period there is further cause for dissatisfaction in respect of similar misconduct/continued poor performance to that described above, it may result in your dismissal from employment. It is hoped that this warning will lead to an immediate, substantial and sustained level of improvement in your conduct so that such action will not be necessary. *(If relevant, add:)* Please note that this final written (stage 3) warning has been issued to you as the first stage of the company's disciplinary procedure given the seriousness of your conduct.

This letter will be placed on your personal file for the duration of the warning. When the warning has expired it will then be removed from your file. In accordance with our data protection policy, the human resources department will keep a record of this warning.

You have the right to appeal against this decision if you are not satisfied with it. If you do wish to appeal, you must inform the company in writing of the reason for your appeal within *(X)* days, in accordance with the company's disciplinary procedure, a copy of which is attached for your information. If you do appeal, the company will then invite you to attend an appeal hearing which you must take all reasonable steps to attend.

Yours sincerely,

(Name)
Line Manager

Please sign and return a copy of this final written warning letter to indicate that you have received it and understand its contents.

Signed: ....   Date:

....
(Name of employee)

APPENDIX III

Letter J

Confirmation of Dismissal with Notice

(Date)

(Name)
(Address)

Dear *(Name)*

CONFIRMATION OF DISMISSAL WITH NOTICE

Further to your disciplinary hearing which was conducted by *(name)*, held on *(date)* regarding *(details of incident)* on *(date)*, this letter confirms the termination of your contract of employment. You are entitled to receive *(number)* weeks'/months' notice of termination of your employment. You *are/are not* required to work out your notice period. We, therefore, confirm that the date of termination of your employment will be *(date)*. This is your last day of service with the company.

At the hearing you were given the statutory right to be accompanied and you chose to *waive this right/have in attendance (name)*.

As you know, a full investigation of the facts surrounding the complaint against you was made. Having put the specific facts to you for your comment at the disciplinary hearing, it was decided that your explanation was not acceptable in the circumstances. For this reason and in consideration of a previous active final written warning you received for similar misconduct/poor performance, the company believes it is left with no alternative other than to dismiss you with notice from its employment on the grounds of misconduct/continued poor performance. The company would refer you to the following aspects of your conduct/performance that are, in the company's view, unacceptable and which have led to your dismissal:

- *(List each of the complaints, which have resulted in the employee's dismissal).*

Your P45 will be sent to you in due course and you will be paid the following amounts:

(a) All pay up to and including the effective date of termination of your employment.
(b) Notice pay *(only if the employee is to be paid in lieu of their notice period).*
(c) Accrued holiday pay *(if applicable, you can even 'claw back' pay if too much holiday has been taken).*

You have the right to appeal against this decision if you are not satisfied with it. If you do wish to appeal, you must inform the company in writing, stating the reason for your appeal, within (*X*) days in accordance with the company's disciplinary procedure, a copy of which is attached for your information. If you do appeal, the company will then invite you to attend an appeal hearing which you must take all reasonable steps to attend.

Yours sincerely,

(Name)
Line Manager

Enc

APPENDIX III

Letter K

Confirmation of Summary Dismissal for Gross Misconduct

(Date)

(Name)
(Address)

Dear *(Name)*

CONFIRMATION OF SUMMARY DISMISSAL FOR GROSS MISCONDUCT

Further to your disciplinary hearing which was conducted by *(name)*, held on *(date)*, regarding *(details of incident)* on *(date)*, this letter confirms the termination of your contract of employment without notice with effect from *(date)*. This is your last day of service with the company.

At the hearing you were given the statutory right to be accompanied and you chose to *waive this right/have in attendance (name)*.

As you know, a full investigation of the facts surrounding the complaint against you was made by *(name)*. Having put the specific facts to you for your comment at the disciplinary hearing, it was decided that your explanation was not acceptable in the circumstances. For this reason, the company believes it is left with no alternative other than to summarily dismiss you from its employment on the grounds of gross misconduct. The gravity of your misconduct is such that the company believes the trust and confidence placed in you as its employee have been completely undermined. The company would refer you to the following aspects of your conduct which are, in the company's view, wholly unacceptable and which have led to your summary dismissal:

- *(List each of the gross misconduct complaints which have resulted in the employee's summary dismissal).*

Your P45 will be sent to you in due course and you will be paid the following amounts:

(a) All pay up to and including the effective date of termination of your employment.
(b) Accrued holiday pay *(if applicable).*

You have the right to appeal against this decision if you are not satisfied with it. If you do wish to appeal, you must inform the company in writing, stating the reason for your appeal, within (*X*) days in accordance with the company's disciplinary procedure, a copy of which is attached for your information. If you do appeal, the company will then invite you to attend an appeal hearing which you must take all reasonable steps to attend.

Yours sincerely,

(Name)
Line Manager

Enc

APPENDIX III

Letter L

Notification of a Disciplinary Appeal Hearing

(Date)

(Name)
(Address)

Dear *(Name)*

NOTIFICATION OF A DISCIPLINARY APPEAL HEARING

We refer to your letter dated *(date)* in which you lodged an appeal against the *formal verbal warning/first written warning/final written warning/termination of your contract of employment* confirmed to you in our letter dated *(date).*

Your appeal against the disciplinary decision will be heard at an appeal hearing to take place on *(date)* at *(time)* at *(location). The appeal hearing will be chaired by (name – the appeal should be heard by a Senior Executive or a Director not previously involved in the procedure).*

You have the statutory right to be accompanied at the appeal hearing. Your companion may be either a fellow employee or a trade union representative of your choice. Your companion will be permitted to address the hearing and to confer with you during the hearing but they will not be permitted to answer questions on your behalf. You should inform the chair of the appeal hearing in advance of the identity of your chosen companion.

If you would like to submit a written statement detailing your grounds for appeal for consideration in advance of the appeal hearing, you may do so. This should be forwarded to *(name – the*

Executive or Director hearing the appeal). At the appeal hearing, you will of course be given an opportunity to set out the detailed grounds for your appeal, including providing any new evidence or new facts on which you may wish to rely.

If you or your chosen companion is unable to attend this appeal hearing, you are asked to contact *(name – the Executive or Director hearing the appeal)* as a matter of urgency so that an alternative date and time can be scheduled. You are reminded that you are required to take all reasonable steps to attend the appeal hearing. Failure to attend without good reason could result in the hearing being held, and a decision being taken, in your absence. However, if you fail to attend through circumstances completely outside your control and which are currently unforeseeable, the company will arrange another appeal hearing. Thereafter, if you fail to attend for a second time without good reason, the hearing will be held, and a decision will be taken on your appeal, in your absence.

After the hearing, you will be informed in writing of the company's decision. Please note that the decision made following this appeal hearing will be final and there will be no further right of appeal against it.

Yours sincerely,

(Name)
Line Manager

APPENDIX III

Letter M

Confirmation of the Outcome of a Disciplinary Appeal Hearing

(Date)

(Name)
(Address)

Dear *(Name)*

OUTCOME OF THE DISCIPLINARY APPEAL HEARING

Further to the appeal hearing which was conducted by *(name)*, held on *(date)* relating to the *formal verbal warning/first written warning/final written warning/termination of your contract of employment* confirmed to you in our letter dated *(date)*, the company has now taken a decision on your appeal, namely that the original disciplinary decision is *upheld/withdrawn/to be reviewed/replaced with a lesser warning (ie. Formal Verbal Warning/ First Written Warning/Final Written Warning)*.

The reasons for this decision are as follows:

- *(List reasons for the decision)*.

You have now exercised your right of appeal under the company's disciplinary procedure and this decision is final.

Yours sincerely,

(Name)
(Chief Executive/Director)

APPENDIX IV

Checklist 1

Formal or Informal Warning?

A GUIDE

There are significant procedural differences between formal and informal disciplinary meetings. Much of this would be considered as best practice, some of it required by employment laws. The failure to follow the legal guidelines or indeed the ACAS Code of Practice on handling disciplinary matters is very likely to have an impact on the outcome at any tribunal.

The following lists (which are not necessarily exhaustive) contain some of the issues to be aware of.

Formal Warnings	Informal Warnings
The right to be accompanied (by a colleague or a trade union representative).	The meeting will normally be on a one to one basis.
If any disciplinary sanctions are to be imposed the meeting must adopt a formal style. Sanctions would include a formal warning, a suspension without pay, demotion, downgrading etc.	No disciplinary sanctions should be imposed. An action plan or improvement plan could be agreed.
For minor offences an informal meeting should have been held before a formal hearing is convened.	

Formal Warnings	Informal Warnings
The formal process will follow a stage-by-stage approach. For example, if a stage 1 (verbal) warning is issued and the improvement sought is not evident, the employee will be moved to stage 2 (a written warning).	It is possible for a number of informal discussions to be held with an employee for the same reason. It must be made clear to the employee when this informal process has reached its conclusion. Managers/ supervisors must inform the employee that a failure to improve after the last informal chat will result in formal action being required.
It is good practice to write to the employee outlining that there will be a formal meeting. Adequate time should be given in advance of the meeting. Evidence of the alleged offence should be provided to the employee, again well in advance of the disciplinary meeting. An employee has the legal right to request a delay of up to five working days if their chosen representative is temporarily not available.	No notice is required for an informal discussion. An employee can be asked to pop in to the manager's office and the informal meeting can take place immediately.
Any formal warning or sanction will be recorded. This means that a letter or e-mail will be sent to the employee and a copy will be placed on their record.	A simple follow up note may be made – for example an improvement plan or action list. However, remember this is meant to be informal and the outcome should not be formally recorded – for example in the employee's personnel file. It is acceptable (and indeed is good practice) for the supervisor/line manager to make a diary note of the conversation.

Formal Warnings	Informal Warnings
Any formal warning/sanction must be accompanied by the right to appeal.	It is not customary, and certainly not a legal requirement, that an appeal be offered following any informal discussion.
It is good practice to always adjourn the formal meeting before deciding on a verdict or an outcome.	
Formal warnings will be accompanied by a warning letter which should indicate the duration of the warning and any review periods set.	Informal warnings do not generally have a set duration period in company policies. It would be good practice to agree a review date with the individual.
Only formal warnings can be taken into consideration in a redundancy exercise. It is permissible for disciplinary sanctions to be taken into consideration when deciding whom to select for redundancy.	Informal warnings should be disregarded in any redundancy selection procedures.
The presence of an HR professional, or the calling of any witnesses, make any disciplinary hearing formal.	As mentioned this should be a one to one interview, unless there are exceptional circumstances.
There should be a full investigation carried out prior to any formal hearing. There may even need to be a preliminary investigation meeting.	Whilst a full investigation is not normally required prior to an informal chat, there should still be a 'fact finding' exercise. Even for an informal discussion, it is important for the manager/supervisor to have the facts available. This is after all a discussion of someone's poor performance, attendance or misconduct, even if this is minor.

APPENDIX IV

Checklist 2

Preparation for a Disciplinary Hearing

The following represents a comprehensive but not exhaustive checklist that can be used prior to a formal disciplinary hearing. This is not required when contemplating an informal discussion. Clearly not everything on this list will be relevant on each occasion. The items are not listed in order of importance.

First of all, conduct a thorough investigation to include factors such as:

- What is the age and length of service of the employee?

- Is a copy of the offer letter/contract of employment required?

- Why do you want to hold a disciplinary hearing – what are your objectives? Remember the aim is normally to close the gap between standards and actual conduct/performance – it is not just to issue a warning. What outcome do you want?

- Are the company's standards clear – can I prove the employee was aware of these standards?

- Is it clear what the employee is alleged to have done or failed to do?

- Have clear evidence (facts) of a gap between the expected level of performance or conduct and the level actually delivered by the employee. This means an investigation has taken place.

- Are there any witnesses – is this fact or hearsay? Obtain written witness statements where relevant.

- When conducting an investigatory meeting with the employee concerned, write to them (see Appendix III: Letter B) ensuring that you offer a companion. If they choose to be accompanied, ask the employee who will be representing them.

- Obtain facts about the disciplinary circumstances, for example:

    - what happened?
    - when did it happen?
    - who was involved?
    - where did the incident occur, etc? Do I need to visit the location?

- What job is being done by the employee – is this their normal job? Do I need a copy of the job description?

- Do I need a copy of the training record?

- Do I need a copy of the induction checklist?

- How long has the employee been in the present job?

- Has the job changed in any way recently?

- Have the standards been changed recently?

- Review the employee's previous disciplinary history making sure to pick up any formal live warnings, but expired warnings should normally be disregarded.

- Has the employee been spoken to before about their poor performance/poor conduct? When was this? Do you have a record? Was this formal or informal?

- Do you have a record of any informal verbal warnings given?

- Are there any culture/race/diversity issues? – this may influence appropriate representation or affect the disciplinary decision making.

- Are there any disability issues? – should I have made any reasonable adjustments to the standard? Are any adjustments needed for the hearing itself?

- Was any injury or damage caused during the incident?

- What do the company's rules and procedures say will happen here?

- Have I issued the employee with the latest copy of the Disciplinary Procedure?

- Does the employee know what stage of the process we are now at?

- Have I followed the rules of natural justice?

- Are there any outstanding grievances from this employee? If so, deal with these first.

Once your investigation is completed you will then need to consider the following:

- Is a disciplinary hearing the next course of action based on the findings from the investigation? If not inform the employee in writing (see Appendix III: Letter C).

- If proceeding with a disciplinary hearing provide advance written notice of the hearing (see Appendix III: Letter D), making sure the employee is aware of the specific allegations and their statutory rights. Have I given them an opportunity to see the evidence against them before the disciplinary hearing in order for them to prepare their case?

- Decide who will accompany you at the disciplinary hearing. What roles will you be playing? Who will take notes?

- If you intend to tape record the disciplinary hearing, plan this well in advance and inform all concerned.

- Does the person need any particular type of support for the disciplinary hearing due to any disability or language issues?

- Have I organised the venue?

- Does the venue offer privacy?

- There may be adjournments – do I need a separate room to break out to?

- Assert control by laying out the interview room to suit your purposes – what are you trying to achieve? Do you go for formal/informal?

- Do I need to organise refreshments?

- Have tissues available! Remove sharp objects from the desk!!

- When you are ready to begin the hearing, go and collect the employee and their representative (if accompanied) from reception. Start with positive introductions... and good luck!

APPENDIX IV

Checklist 3

Carrying Out a Disciplinary Hearing

The following represents a checklist of the main stages you should go through when conducting a formal disciplinary hearing. This is not required when contemplating an informal discussion.

- Explain who are present and their role in the disciplinary hearing.

- Ensure a clear record of the disciplinary hearing is taken.

- Confirm that the employee was given the right to be accompanied.

- Where applicable, confirm that the employee has been given access to information gathered during investigations including statements taken, and has had sufficient opportunity to consider the content.

- Explain how the disciplinary hearing will proceed.

- Give all the reasons for the disciplinary hearing and the facts established during the investigation.

- Give the employee the right to reply to each allegation.

- Indicate that you are about to adjourn to make your decision; ask employee and companion for any final comments.

- Adjourn to discuss and make a decision based on the facts and the employee's response. Consider not only the company policy but also ask yourself 'what normally happens here?' (custom and practice). Write down your decision as a record.

- Reconvene.

- Give the outcome, perhaps reading from the prepared statement made in the adjournment. (avoid further debate on the issues).

- Where applicable, agree with the employee what action, targets, performance is required.

- If applicable, confirm the date for a follow-up review meeting.

- Explain the appeal procedure.

- Explain that a letter will follow confirming the outcome of the disciplinary hearing and the appeal procedure.

- Explain that a written record of the interview will also be given to the employee and representative (if accompanied).

APPENDIX IV

Checklist 4

Formal Warning Letter Content

Items to be included in formal warning letters are as follows:

(a) Ensure the warning letter is dated. Also clarify the date of commencement of the warning period.

(b) The warning letter should refer to the disciplinary hearing (*attach a copy of the minutes if available?*). Clarify whether the employee was accompanied, and if so, by whom. If the employee opted to be unrepresented, include this in the letter.

(c) Warning letters must contain clear and specific instructions as to the action required by the individual in order to meet the standards that the company requires; ie achieve this target or standard by this date etc.

(d) It is important to point out to the employee what stage has been reached in the disciplinary process.

(e) Warning letters should contain clear guidance as to what happens next if the employee fails to attain the standards of performance or conduct required within the time period stated.

(f) It is good practice for warning letters to refer to the company's own disciplinary rules and procedures. Wordings similar to 'in accordance with the company's disciplinary procedure we consider this to be a serious breach of conduct, and as the procedure indicates, this results in the issue of a formal written warning'.

(g) It is vital that warning letters state clearly how long the warning is to last. Consider putting the expiry date of the warning in the letter so that this is clear. The letter should also indicate that the performance or conduct will be reviewed at regular intervals during the warning period.

(h) Warning letters must refer to an appeal procedure. This is an important issue. Warning letters must contain an outline of the right of appeal, confirm to whom the appeal should be made, and by when; it is also worth asking the employee to confirm the grounds for the appeal.

(i) A copy of any warning letter must be placed on the individual's personal file (In view of the employment rights contained in the Data Protection Act and the Human Rights Act, it would now be good practice to indicate how long the warning will remain on the person's file and point out what will happen to the warning after it has expired).

APPENDIX IV

Checklist 5

Investigations Checklist

HOW SERIOUS IS IT?

An investigation must establish the seriousness of the alleged misconduct and be proportionate to it. So, your response may range from a brief discussion with the employee to establish the facts, to a full-scale investigation involving other agencies such as the police. The objective should be to provide sound factual evidence for any subsequent disciplinary action. Investigators should ask themselves what they can reasonably expect to achieve given the time and resources available. Any internal investigation should follow the LIFT principle – it should be logical, impartial, fair and time-bound.

Remember that the evidence does not have to be sufficient to prove the allegations (to a criminal standard). After a thorough investigation the employer must have formed a genuine belief that the misconduct occurred – on the balance of probability (the civil standard of proof , in other words, more likely than not that it happened).

WHO CONDUCTS IT?

Ideally those conducting the investigation should not also hear the disciplinary complaint. It is not unlawful if they do, but would not be considered good practice in most situations. These two functions should be kept separate in the interests of natural justice. Tribunals and the ACAS Code of Practice on disciplinary and grievance procedures acknowledge this will not always be possible, especially for small businesses (www.acas. org.uk). Even so, if funds permit, employers should consider using an independent investigator for more serious cases. For larger organisations, it is important that HR and the investigating manager work together. Protocols need to be agreed and good communications maintained throughout the investigation.

KEEP AN OPEN MIND

Do not assume guilt or innocence. Decide whether the employee should be suspended on full pay during the investigation. Make sure this is described as a precautionary measure – it should be made clear it is not a disciplinary sanction. Such action should only be considered in more serious cases (gross misconduct is suspected) where the employee's continued presence in the workplace might have a disruptive effect or enable employees to undermine the case against them (use Letter A found in Appendix III).

WHAT EVIDENCE SHOULD BE COLLECTED?

Identify the types of evidence you need to gather. Don't rely merely on witness statements. Think about gathering files, documents, and CCTV footage or computer records, if available. Policy documents, induction and training records can also be used. If any evidence is likely to perish or be removed, gather it as a priority. Decide who you need to interview and conduct the interview as soon as possible before memories fade. You are entitled to interview the employee against whom the allegation has been made, but it should be made clear it is an exploratory interview and not a disciplinary hearing (as such there is no right to a companion but do not refuse this unreasonably). Identify what you need to establish from each interviewee and prepare accordingly. It is not advisable to have a pre-prepared list of questions, as you may need to explore particular responses in more detail during the interview. It is better to prepare a list of topics and decide on the order in which you wish to deal with them. Write down the responses given to the questions.

MAKE FULL NOTES WHEN INTERVIEWING

At the end they should be invited to read through the notes and sign them. Draft statements should be taken back to the witness for signature and the notes on which the statement was based retained until the conclusion of any disciplinary hearing or subsequent appeal. Don't put words into witnesses' mouths with 'leading questions' or suggest answers. Your questions should encourage them to recall their version of events in their own words.

Witnesses should be informed at the end of the interview that if the case results in a disciplinary hearing, they may be required to give evidence. They need to be aware that anonymity cannot be guaranteed unless there is a genuine fear of reprisal, or similar justification.

CRIMINAL ACTIVITY

Some of the more serious allegations of misconduct may potentially be criminal offences. If you suspect this is the case, you may need to inform other agencies – for example, the Health and Safety Executive, Revenue/ Customs or the police. The evidence you gather for your internal investigation may also be required for a parallel criminal investigation. If this is the case, continuity of evidence is important. For your evidence to be admissible in a criminal prosecution, you need to be able to demonstrate its physical location at any point in time.

Seek legal advice at an early stage on how continuity can best be achieved.

If an employee admits to a criminal offence during the course of an internal investigation, it is advisable to make a note of it in case it needs to be used as evidence in any subsequent criminal proceedings. The note should be timed, dated and signed by the person taking it and the employee should read and sign it. Where the employee disagrees with the record, note the details and ask them to read and sign them to the effect that they accurately reflect the disagreement. Any refusal to sign should also be recorded. The investigation should then be terminated with a view to involving the police or any other appropriate investigatory body. Failure to do this is likely to make such unsolicited comments inadmissible in a criminal court.

CONCLUDING THE INVESTIGATION

Once you feel you have sufficient evidence on which to base a decision, finish the investigation. The standard of proof for most internal investigations and any subsequent disciplinary hearing will need only to be on the balance of probabilities. Remember you do not have to prove your case beyond reasonable doubt for it to stand up in a tribunal.

APPENDIX IV

Checklist 6

Persistent Poor Performance

- Is the poor performance due to misconduct or is it a lack of ability? (Won't or Can't?)

- Is the performance poor enough to justify disciplinary action?

- What is the evidence?

- Are there any mitigating circumstances?

- Was the person fully aware of the expected level of job performance?

    - Was this expressed in terms that are clear and leave no room for doubt?
    - Has the person had the appropriate training and support?
    - Is the person suffering from any personal or medical problems that you are aware of?
    - Have other employees performed just as poorly and not been disciplined?
    - Does the individual accept their under performance or not?

- Check your disciplinary procedure.

- Check your disciplinary rules – what do they say will happen to people who under perform?

- Call an interview as quickly as possible after deciding that further informal counselling will serve no useful purpose.

- Make it clear to the person that this is going to be a formal disciplinary meeting as laid down in your procedures. It is not just another informal pep talk.

- Decide who should be present at the interview besides you and the employee. Once you are in the formal disciplinary procedure, the employee must be allowed to be accompanied by a work colleague or union representative. You should consider who would accompany yourself.

- Make sure you have all the necessary evidence and paperwork to hand.

- Remind yourself to approach the interview with an open mind. Remember that the prime purpose of the meeting is to help the person to improve. You must aim to bridge the gap between their current level of performance and the standards expected.

APPENDIX IV

Checklist 7

Qualifying Periods for Unfair Dismissal

If a person is dismissed and wishes to take his/her claim to an Employment Tribunal, there are two initial hurdles to be overcome:

a) Is the person an employee, employed under a contract of employment? (Workers, casual or agency staff, without an employment contract, cannot normally claim unfair dismissal. There are other groups that are excluded, for example police officers and the self-employed)

b) Does the individual have one year's continuous service?

Employers may, therefore, on occasions, be tempted to dismiss employees who have less than one year's service. This is in the mistaken belief that the employee has no employment protection. This would be a serious mistake to make. Employees now enjoy a wide range of protection from the day they commence employment – there is certainly no requirement for a year's service for these issues.

Some of the issues to be wary of are included in the following checklist. Before dismissing employees for any of the following reasons take advice from the HR department or a legal adviser.

Checklist

Dismissal – no service required. This list is not exhaustive:

- A dismissal connected with race, sex, religion, sexual orientation, age or disability discrimination.

- A dismissal connected with a woman's pregnancy, decision to adopt or for taking maternity leave.

- A dismissal connected with trade union membership (or non-membership) or activities.

- A dismissal where the individual refuses to exceed the Working Time Regulations by signing an opt out.

- A dismissal of an individual for raising a genuine health and safety concern or where the person left or proposed to leave the workplace because they felt in serious or imminent danger.

- A dismissal connected with the person's activities as an occupational pension scheme trustee.

- A dismissal connected with an individual's activities as a Safety Representative.

- A dismissal where someone makes a protected disclosure under the Public Interest Disclosure Act, better known as the 'whistle blowers' legislation. Dismissals in the category also carry unlimited compensation.

- A dismissal because the individual asserts his/her rights under the Minimum Wage Act.

- A dismissal where a protected shop worker refuses to work on a Sunday.

- A dismissal connected with an employee's attempt to obtain one of their statutory rights. Clearly if individuals are given statutory rights, a dismissal where someone seeks to assert one of those rights must be considered unfair. Some of these statutory rights include payment of wages and deductions from pay (Wages Act); notice periods; seeking a statement of terms and conditions or requesting unpaid time off to carry out a public duty.

- A dismissal of an individual who is engaged in official industrial action (a strike or work to rule for example) – during the first twelve weeks of the action.

- A claim connected with breach of contract or wrongful dismissal. Claims are limited to £25,000 at Employment Tribunal and can only be commenced on the termination of the contract (but note that such claims can also be taken to the civil courts where these restrictions do not apply).

- A dismissal related to a spent conviction under the Rehabilitation of Offenders Act.

- An instant dismissal, where the employer has failed to follow a contractual disciplinary procedure (This could be a breach of the Human Rights Act as the individual may argue they have been denied the right to a fair hearing, although this appears to be unlikely).

- A dismissal for a reason connected with part-time working.

- A dismissal for taking reasonable leave in an emergency situation involving a dependant.

- A dismissal connected with a person's activities as an employee representative on a European Works Council.

- A dismissal connected with a person's activities as an employee representative in a collective redundancy or business transfer situation.

- A dismissal because the worker took action to secure a benefit under the Tax Credits Act 1999.

- A redundancy, where the reason for selection for redundancy would constitute unfair dismissal (for example, pregnancy).

This checklist is not exhaustive, but it can clearly be seen that employees enjoy a significant amount of protection which commences from their first day at work.

NOTE: Under Transfer Regulations (TUPE), all employees, irrespective of service, acquire the right to be transferred. However one year's service is required for an unfair dismissal claim arising from TUPE.

Index

About the Authors

DEREK ECCLESTON

Derek is an experienced, practical consultant, specia[...] the provision of advice and training on employment [...] employee relations, through his consultancy Emp[...] Law Training Ltd.

He has spent over 25 years in senior HR roles in [...] of industries which include local government (wh[...] initially a Union Rep for NALGO), engineering an[...] services. Derek also worked for 6 years in a law firm, [...] created a unique blend of practical awareness, pr[...] skills and legal expertise.

He is a Fellow of the Chartered Institute of Pe[...] Development (FCIPD), a Chartered Insurer (AC[...] Masters Degree in Employment Law from Leices[...] Derek is a regular presenter for some leading [...] Employment training such as the CIPD, JSB [...] advises smaller enterprises on HR issues and [...] presents public and in-house events.

He is a personal tutor on the CIPD's Advanced Certificate in Employment Law, and is an author of several Employment Law publications.

Derek created a website which provides a comprehensive guide for employees and workers on their rights at work (www.yourjobrights.co.uk) and he updates this site regularly.

Derek Eccleston MA FCIPD ACII
01789 470700
www.eltraining.co.uk

KATE GOSCHEN

Kate, of HR Remedies based in Stratford-upon-Avon, is an experienced and qualified consultant with excellent technical employment law knowledge. She prides herself on her practical application having spent the first 10 years of her career in senior HR roles within a number of industries including broadcasting and local government.

In 2000 she became a consultant for Croner Consulting, a leading national and international HR/Employment Law consultancy advising companies from all different industries; from sole traders to corporate companies employing thousands of people. She also delivered employment law training courses to clients and was responsible for training existing and new consultants to the company on their in-house comprehensive employment law course.

Four years later Kate left to set up her own consultancy business providing employment law and HR consultancy. To the SME she is the consultant and/or outsourced HR function and to

larger businesses she provides lead advice to the existing HR department.

Aside to this, Kate has presented many employment law update seminars to Association/Federation Annual General Meetings and written numerous articles for HR professional journals. She has also appeared in the *Daily Telegraph* newspaper as 'Ask The Expert' addressing Employment Law Questions and Answers.

www.hr-remedies.co.uk

**If you have found this book useful you may
be interested in other titles from Gower**

Age Discrimination in Employment
Malcolm Sargeant
978 0 566 08774 5

Commoditization and the Strategic Response
Andrew Holmes
978 0 566 08743 1

**Brand Risk:
Adding Risk Literacy to Brand Management**
David Abrahams
978 0 566 08724 0

**Global Project Management:
Communication, Collaboration and
Management Across Borders**
Jean Binder
978 0 566 08706 6

**The Goal:
A Process of Ongoing Improvement
Third Edition**
Eliyahu M. Goldratt and Jeff Cox
Hardback 978 0 566 08664 9
Paperback 978 0 566 08665 4

MBA Management Models
Sue Harding and Trevor Long
987 0 566 08137 8

GOWER